GREENER PASTURES

Also by Andrea Kay

Interview Strategies That Will Get You the Job You Want

Resumes That Will Get You the Job You Want

GREENER PASTURES

HOW TO FIND A JOB IN ANOTHER PLACE

Andrea Kay

ST. MARTIN'S GRIFFIN

NEW YORK

Library of Congress Cataloging-in-Publication Data

Kay, Andrea.
    Greener pastures : how to find a job in another place / Andrea Kay.—1st St. Martin's Griffin ed.
        p.   cm.
    Includes bibliographical references
    ISBN 0-312-19892-2
    1. Job hunting—United States.   2. Moving, Household.   I. Title.
    HF5382.75.U6K39   1999
650.14—dc21   98-56140
                                                                    CIP

First St. Martin's Griffin Edition: May 1999

10   9   8   7   6   5   4   3   2   1

When it comes down to it, this is a book about building and nurturing relationships. So it's dedicated to my mother, who taught me to care about other people and the importance of relationships, and my father, who cares more than anyone knows. To Diana for your friendship. To Nitza, Shana, Tiffany, and Jeremy, my daily sustenance. And to Greg, who, every day, teaches me how to be sensitive to others.

Contents

Acknowledgments.................................... ix

Introduction xi

1. Why Go to All That Trouble?.................. 1

2. What You Can Do from Home 21

3. Line Up Your Cheerleaders.................... 57

4. Plotting Your First Visit........................ 89

5. Round One..115

6. How to Be a Nice Nag..........................137

7. They Want You...................................175

8. Finding Your Way at Work and Home........199

Appendix: Helpful Resources......................207

Acknowledgments

If it weren't for the following people, well, who knows how this book would have turned out. They were teeming with information and generous with their time, and I thank you:

Pete Packer, Runzheimer International; David Hoguet, Globe Business Resources; Tom Mackowiak, Location Guides; folks at the Employment Relocation Council; Jennifer Heidlage, West Shell Realty; Barry Lawrence, Society for Human Resources Management; Mary Holdcraft, Career Management Resources; Craig Cox, editor, and Andrea Martin, librarian, *Utne Reader*; Margaret Duerksen, Hoover's Inc.; Kim Lewis, American Sales Leads; Jennifer Kainweller; Corbin Ball, HMR Associates; Joe Mehl, Management Recruiters International; folks at the Internal Revenue Service who couldn't be identified without going through a lot of red tape; Barbara Williams and the two Bonnies at the U.S. Census Bureau; Eric Figueroa at the U.S. Bureau of Labor Statistics; Susan Shore; Ron and Sarah Crossland; Lisa Schwartz; Jeff Krys; Paul Tarai; Daniel Epstein; Bill Merriam; Gordon and Faith Rothman.

Special thanks to Rosemary Deitzer and Michele Naylor, organizers and researchers extraordinaire; Joy Dill, for your professional input and critique and for being my cheerleader; Heather Jackson, for being excited about the project; Carrie McGinnis, for your fine tuning and making sure the book is the best it can be; Andrea Pedolsky, for giving me the idea to explore in the first place, your support and special friendship; Greg Newberry, for all your support and for leaving me alone to write.

Introduction

Something must be going on in your life that's motivating you to want to live and work in a new location. Otherwise, you wouldn't have picked up this book, right?

I sure hope your motive falls under my "Good reasons to move" tally sheet as opposed to my "Not-so-great reasons to move" list that I get into early on in the book. Because looking for a job in a new place, then moving there, is no small feat.

In fact, it can be a big pain in the you-know-what. Whether you're a recent college graduate, veteran of the business world, or partner of someone who's accepted a transfer or new job, you've got a different set of issues facing you in a long-distance job search.

For one thing, you may not know anybody in the place you want to go. So how are you going to find out about job openings? It's like trying to find the proverbial needle in a haystack. Where do you start? How do you make any progress when you aren't even living there?

If you're relying on recruiters and job postings on the Internet, well, good luck. I'm not saying you *can't* find a job those ways. But for one thing, thousands of other people are thinking the same way as you. So you've got lots of competition. And believe it or not, most jobs—the really good ones—aren't listed *anywhere*. You've got to sniff them out yourself, or create them. You've got to be smarter than the average bear.

Even if you're just toying with the idea of looking for a job in another area, *Greener Pastures* will first help you define your motivation and what you need to hash over to decide where to move and work and what you're looking for in a new locale. Then if you're ready to go forward, you'll learn how to start digging up more information about your potential destination and how to search for a job strategically, in a practical detail-by-detail way.

Now, let's say it wasn't your idea to move, but your partner, or your partner's company, decided he or she is relocating, and you'd like to be with them. So you would be reading this book to find a job for yourself in this predetermined locale that you're moving to, thanks to somebody else. *Greener Pastures* is also written with you in mind.

Just to give you an idea of what you'll learn from this book, let's walk through the chapters.

In Chapter 1 I help you define your motivation, understand what you're in for, and who such a move will affect and how.

Since looking for the right job in a place you don't live is ten times harder than a regular job search, you'll need to do research and have a plan. Without it, you'll spend thousands of dollars on airplane tickets, car rentals and gasoline; hundreds on postage and telephone calls; and weeks of your own precious time—with little to show for it. You're going to learn step-by-step how to avoid all that in Chapters 2 and 3.

Two chapters just on that? You won't believe how much research and planning you can do—all from the comforts of home, which is really the crux of your long-distance job search. See, the key to your success in finding this job you want—not just any old job—will be to have a clear goal and savvy strategy, know exactly whom you want to talk to and how you're going to contact them, especially when you're trying to nudge your way into a new community. *People* are going to be your gold mine.

So you'll learn how to connect with people you know, people you don't know but want to know, and how to enlist their help. Also, you'll find out how to talk about yourself and discover potential jobs—through real people as well as through other sources.

After Chapters 2 and 3, you're ready to visit your targeted market to talk to people about the area, get acquainted with the business climate, get the scoop on specific companies, hold job interviews, potentially dig up job opportunities, and let people see why they'd love to have you at their company. Almost. First you need to read Chapter 4.

This is where you learn how to create your Move Manifesto, just one of the unique approaches to a long-distance job search that will make this an organized, well-planned venture. I also help you prepare for meetings you're going to hold with key decision makers—whom I'll show you how to get to. I also have some juicy little tips on how to keep your trip cheap.

Once you're visiting your desired location, you'll appreciate Chapter 5, which helps you prioritize what's what. I've tried to anticipate everything you might encounter—like, What if you discover a job opening? What if you have the opportunity to create a position for yourself? What if things aren't going well? How can you explore optional working arrangements if you're determined to move without a job?

Now comes the hard part—what you do once you're back home and out of sight, out of mind. This is where you learn how to be a Nice Nag. How to stay in the forefront of people's minds. How to make sure they only think of you when they're wondering: Who should I hire for this new position? Who's the perfect fit? And, finally, what do you do when it's been three weeks and there are no offers? What do you do when it's been two months and no bites? How do you stay motivated? It's all in Chapter 6.

Chapter 7 is where we assume you've gotten an offer (which you *will* eventually get)—maybe even two or three—and now you have to figure out whether you want it or which one to take. You'll learn how to evaluate an offer. How to get what you want—salary and otherwise. I also get you thinking about move-related issues like tax write-offs, how to break the news to your employer if you're employed—and what you tell all the people who have helped you along the way.

Then Chapter 8 gets into how to get settled once you've moved: dealing with items such as kids and unemployed partners—some of the many issues that can crop up.

At the end of the book you'll find lists of books, web sites, telephone numbers, addresses, and resources that will save you time, energy, and money in your search.

You've probably figured out by now that *Greener Pastures* is written chronologically—in the order in which you would conduct a long-distance job search. It's the only way that makes sense, don't you think? So you'll want to start at the beginning and go from there. No skipping chapters. Otherwise you'll miss important stuff.

This brings me to one more major point. Looking for a job in another location is a process. All the steps I get into here are part of that process. *Greener Pastures* will help you prepare and position yourself for this unique process. It can help you cut your job search time in half.

If you're wondering how many other people like you are out there, well, no one seems to know exactly. Something like eighteen million households move each year (the latest figures for 1995 from the Census Bureau, who are very nice folks, I might add). And it looks like out of those, some 2,097,000 households moved for a new job.

But what's the difference anyway? Whether it's two million or twelve million. Something is going on in *your* life that's motivating you to want to live and work in a new location. Remember, that's why you picked up this book in the first place. So now let's find out the best way for you to achieve that goal.

1

WHY GO TO ALL THAT TROUBLE?

There's only one good reason to pack up and move to a new place to live and work: it makes perfect sense to you and the people in your life who are affected.

It does not matter what anyone else thinks, whether they would do it themselves or even if they understand your rationale. Whose life is it anyway? This is a good time to mention the fact that the average life expectancy is seventy-three years. That can go by pretty quick. So while you're here on earth, I'd urge you to live your life the way *you* want. I was going to wait awhile before I started dropping those kinds of helpful, life-saving tips, but, hey, there's no time like the present.

Now that we got that straight, let's talk about what a perfectly good reason to move might be.

People rarely move just for the heck of it. It's too much work. All that packing and sorting through papers, books, kitchen paraphernalia, clothes, and bathroom stuff you've had for eons. Plus you've got your routine, your favorite breakfast spots, pharmacy, doctors, and so on. Not to mention how costly it is. The average move costs around $47,000 if you own a home. Can you believe it? It can also be risky. What if things don't work out the way you planned? No, siree, you don't want to be making a move unless something significant is motivating you.

SOME PERFECTLY GOOD REASONS TO MOVE

- You've been offered a job *you want*, you'll be compensated well for your contribution and, overall, the job is an excellent fit.
- *You want* to be geographically closer to family, friends, or someone you have a relationship with.
- *You want* to live in a community that is more conducive to your values and activities.
- *You want* to be in an area that, due to the environment or climate, allows you to incorporate recreational or cultural activities that are a key part of your life.
- *You want* to live in a climate that is healthier for you or a loved one.
- *You want* to reside in an area where business is good for your line of work or industry is more plentiful.
- *You want* to be with your spouse or significant other who is moving for a job.

All of the above reasons show that you are clear on your values and priorities at this time in your life. You have defined what you want. (Notice that all of them have the words "you want" in them.) A geographical move will help you meet your long- or short-term goal.

However, that is not to say that you won't have misgivings or vacillate as to whether moving is a good, bad, or mediocre idea. You will. For instance, you may *love* living in Los Angeles, where you've been for the last ten years, but you want to be near your seventy-year-old mother, who lives in Cleveland.

So expect to have conversations like the one that follows between you and your best friend sipping non-fat lattes in your favorite Santa Monica coffee house:

You: I'm thinking about moving back to Cleveland to be near my mother.

YOUR BEST FRIEND: Wow. That's a big decision. Are you sure about that?

YOU: Of course not. I love Santa Monica. All I have to do is walk outside my apartment and there are fifteen things to do. The ocean is ten blocks away. My friends are all here. My job is here. It snows in Cleveland. I don't know a soul there anymore, except my cousin Karen and Melanie Shebowksi, my best friend from seventh grade. And I probably won't like her anymore.

YOUR BEST FRIEND: So how can you do it?

YOU: My mother. She's getting up in years. How much longer will she be around? My brother is three hundred miles away. I just feel like I want to be closer.

Even though you adore L.A., you're willing to move because you've decided that being close to your mother is your priority and, therefore, the determining factor for where to live at this point in your life.

Or what if your company gets bought by some giant conglomerate and they decide to close your office? Since you have to start job hunting, you decide to check out the Southeast, an area of the country you've always liked.

Or let's say you are pleased as punch about living in the Midwest, but because your son has bad allergies, you've decided you need to move to a state with a less humid climate, like Arizona. Perhaps you're comfy and cozy in Milwaukee, but since your spouse has been offered a promotion in St. Louis, and the two of you decided her job takes priority, you're going to move.

It's likely you will have lively, heated, perhaps even tearful discussions with the people in your life that a move like this affects. A geographical move can have great impact on you and your family.

Packing up and moving to a new place to live and work must be *something you want and makes perfectly good sense to you and the people in your life who are affected.*

So when considering a geographical move, hash out the pros and cons to get clear on your priorities. Ultimately, the decision to move will be based on what's important to you and the people closest to you.

NOT-SO-GREAT REASONS

On the other hand, there are some not-so-great reasons for wanting to move. They include the desire to get away from a crummy job, a jerky boss, or any type of perceived failure or the wish to go where no one knows you.

If you move for any of those reasons, you're doing it to get *away* from something. It's as if you're on the lam. You're a fugitive. There's a feeling of unfinished business. When somebody asks why you want to move (and believe me lots of people will ask), unless you make something up, the reasons are negative. You have nothing to look forward to, really. Your move is about getting away.

I had a client who had lived in Ohio his whole life, then moved himself and his family to Florida for a job. The job in Florida didn't work out. To say he was disappointed that the job hadn't worked out is putting it mildly—he was devastated by the loss. But instead of dealing with his pain, figuring out what had happened and setting new goals, he tried to move on as quickly as possible. He came home the day he got his pink slip and told his wife, "We're moving back to Ohio, where I know people." Within weeks he took the first job that came along. After three days he knew he made the wrong decision. He kept the job for six months and finally left before he got a new position. Then he was even more distraught.

"I have to stop running," he told me the day he came to see me. "I have to face what happened in Florida and figure out what I really want."

I'm not suggesting that you stay in a bad work situation or

remain in a location you can't tolerate. Just be straight with yourself. Identify what didn't work out and if and how you might have contributed to the situation. Get a clear perspective on what you do want—which might be in another geographical location.

Be able to describe your next career position (or if this is your first) in terms of the:

- Skills you'll use
- Way it will challenge you
- Pay you'll receive
- Environment and management you would like

When you know what you want and can describe it to others, it will be easier to get and to enroll others to help you get it. Make the decision to move for a position that has what you want, not what you want to get away from. See the difference?

WHAT'S YOUR MOTIVATION?

To help clarify the reasons behind your desire to move—even it's just random thought at this point—fill in the following blanks:

I'd like to move because

_____

_____

_____

_____

This is based on my (and my family's; my partner's) priority/priorities to

_____

_____

(Make sure this is something you want to move toward, rather than something you want to get away from.)

Sometimes the last thing in the world you were thinking about was making a move. Then one day you get a phone call from a headhunter telling you about a fabulous opportunity in Maine. What do you do?

I'd give you the same advice I gave to this twenty-something-year-old I met at a book signing I was doing at an airport bookstore a few years ago. He lived in Knoxville and loved it there, but his company wanted him to move to Kansas because someone else was returning to the Knoxville office and would need to take his position. He had the choice of whether to go or not. But he felt his standing in the company would be affected if he didn't make the move. Besides, the move to Kansas would be a promotion. I helped him think through the pros and cons, then told him the following:

If you want to know whether you should make a move, don't ask me. There's only one good reason to pack up and go to a new place to live and work: *it makes perfectly good sense to you and the people in your life who are affected.* Get my point?

KNOW WHAT YOU'RE IN FOR

Most everything in life has an upside and, well, let's call them less than desirable side effects. The biggest upside of making a move to a new location is that you get what you want (that reason that you filled in on page 5.) You get to be close to your seventy-year-old mother. Or you get that senior vice president job you've worked hard for. You have an opportunity that could be a segue into your dream job. You can surround yourself and family with the type of religious community you want. You get to be in a place with a broad cultural and ethnic mix. Or you will be able to breathe healthier air. Whatever.

Depending on your point of view, the change may also offer other advantages. New friends, a safer living environment, a quieter lifestyle, a more exciting life.

The other side of the coin is that a geographical move creates utter upheaval in one's life. Everything changes. And I mean everything. There are new doctors, dry cleaners, churches, synagogues, banks, friends, neighbors, roads, freeways, shortcuts, politics, city government, and weather. You leave behind friends, family, schools, teachers, coworkers, and neighbors.

As one woman who moved for her husband's job put it: "Moving is like 'root shock,' the initial wilting a plant goes through when you remove it from soil and transplant it somewhere else. You have all the main parts—tap root, stem, leaves—but the little hair roots get left behind and the plant shows signs of wilting until it can regrow those rootlets. Family, friends, professional associations, neighborhood, doctors, dentists, and dry cleaners are your rootlets. They have to be reestablished. If you go into the move joyously and well prepared, the wilting only lasts a short time."

Even if you're just out of college, if you don't own a home, or if you're single, moving is a big deal. If you own a home, have children in school, and have lived in a community a long time, moving is even a bigger deal.

◆ **How It Affects Kids**

According to an article written by relocation expert Beverly Roman in *Runzheimer Reports on Relocation*, approximately 9.6 million children between the ages of one and fourteen relocated with their families in 1996. A child's reaction to a move depends on his or her age. Very young kids pretty much tag along. The older the child, though, the tougher the move. Teenagers especially are not keen on leaving their friends and familiar surroundings. Their life is their home, school, family, and friends. A move uproots them from most of that.

Some children are more sensitive to change than others and may have difficulties in school and social settings. Lisa Shaw, author of several books aimed at people who want to move to the country, says: "Kids aren't furniture that can be loaded into a van and moved to a new house . . . children are basically much more conservative than adults. Change for the sake of something new does not appeal to them and they take great comfort in the familiar. Any move requires some special attention to the needs and fears of children."

If you have children and decide to make a move, see Chapter 8 for some tips and Chapter 9 for resources on easing the transition for children.

◆ HOW IT AFFECTS SPOUSES AND PARTNERS

The partner of the person who's moving for a new job usually reacts in one or more of three ways:

1. Angry and resentful.

I know one couple who spent weeks discussing whether to move for his career. They went back and forth. At first she was dead set against it.

"Why should my career be considered second to his?" she asked me. A moment later, she'd say something like, "It's probably for the best since his job has more advancement possibilities."

After weeks of discussion, they decided his job at this major corporation was the primary career in their family right now. They agreed that they'd move. But as the time got closer for her to resign from her job, which she loved, she became angry and resentful.

Now, you may be wondering how that could be. They had discussed it. And they had mutually agreed it was a good idea. Yes, it seemed like a rational move, but she still felt slighted. Can you blame her?

Here's the story of another couple I knew. One of the partners had just taken a full-time position with an organization in their hometown of Boston, after six months of lobbying for it. He had written a proposal, even worked for a month without pay for this organization to show his commitment. Then, unexpectedly, his wife's company offered her a promotion, but it meant she had to transfer to Wisconsin. As much as he wanted her to accept the promotion, he didn't want to give up this new position he had worked so hard to get.

Sometimes people just don't want to give up the things that make them part of their community. Take Leonard, who was a soccer team coach and was pursuing his degree at a college in Pennsylvania. Or Maggie, who was a literacy tutor and volunteer at a retirement home. Both of them felt angry and resentful when their partners wanted to move.

Other times, people make decisions based on what's best for their careers, even when it's not something either partner was pursuing. For example, Fran and Gary were living in Indianapolis, where he worked for a TV station and she managed a women's legal clinic.

"We hadn't been looking to move. But I noticed an item on the news wire about plans for a new cable TV news network to be run jointly by ABC and Westinghouse," explains Gary. "The base of operations was to be Stamford, Connecticut. First I checked an atlas to determine this was not in the New England woods, but an express train ride from New York City. It sounded like a perfect opportunity and could lead to a career as a field producer. I knew that chance wasn't going to present itself as long as I was in Indianapolis.

"We talked about the pros and cons. We'd be giving up a lot of comfort. We both had jobs we were good at, we had friends, and we'd spent a lot of time renovating the bathroom. We were nearly equidistant from Fran's parents in Ohio and mine in Chicago."

When they got married, they had explicitly agreed to move once for him, once for her, so Fran agreed reluctantly to leave Indianapolis.

2. Scared.

Many people have never lived anywhere but thirty miles away from their hometown. The result is that if one spouse wants to move for a new job, the fear of the unknown kicks in: What if that new job doesn't work out? What if things change in, say, two years in the new location? Will we have to move again?

A partner may be afraid he or she won't be able to find a job in the new location at the same level he or she is at now. I know of a few people who sabotaged their partner's job search process (probably not intentionally) because they really didn't want to make a move.

3. Excited.

Other partners are open to an adventure. This seems to be the case more with people who have moved before and aren't living in their native city.

Melanie and Rob, who were in their early thirties, were eager to move after he got laid off from his job in New York.

"We decided this was the opportunity to get away from the cold and move to a warmer climate," they explained. They focused their job searches on the southern part of the U.S. Within six months, he was working for Coca-Cola in Atlanta and she had landed a position at a hospital in the area.

OTHER REACTIONS

Sometimes it is the spouse initiating the move who has second thoughts. He or she may feel guilty about uprooting the family.

A couple may also get pressure from parents, in-laws, and siblings. On few occasions I've seen families who can't understand a couple's decision to relocate to accommodate the *wife's* career.

Fran remembers her father-in-law chastising her for being resentful because "Gary could only do his job in a few places, but I could work anywhere."

◆ HOW IT AFFECTS YOUR POCKET

If you rent a home or apartment, expect your relocation to cost on average $13,638, according to the Employee Relocation Council (using 1997 data). If you own a home, the average cost to relocate is $47,901, according to ERC. Obviously, these costs don't come out of your pocket if your company or your partner's company is paying for your move. But that is not always the case.

Why does it cost so much? Well, it's not like you just up and move. If you own a home, say relocation experts Runzheimer International, you need to pay for such things as shipment and storage of household goods, temporary living at your new location, expenses during home-finding trips, moving automobiles, costs to sell your home, costs to purchase your new home, orientation trips to the new location, and child and elder care. The biggest expenses are the shipping of your household goods and the closing costs on your new home.

And even if you rent, you face many of the same things, as well as the costs of lease breaking, apartment search fees, and security deposits.

The cost of living in a new area might be higher. For example, an 8-room, 2,000-square-foot home with 4 bedrooms and 2.5 baths in Phoenix, Arizona, costs $153,000. In Washington, D.C., the same housing costs $249,200.

Another thing that can affect your pocketbook is if your spouse or partner has to leave a job in order to move with you. You may lose half your family income—at least for awhile.

To help you think through how a move will affect your life and what you'd need to do to make it happen, answer the following questions:

Who will a geographical move affect?

Just me _____ Others _____

Person's name	How it affects him/her	How can we handle or overcome this? How can we ease the transition?
_____	_____	_____
_____	_____	_____
_____	_____	_____
_____	_____	_____
_____	_____	_____
_____	_____	_____
_____	_____	_____

Others issues in my life that are affected by a move:

_____

_____

_____

_____

_____

Don't let any of this scare you from making a move. Just be realistic. Consider everything and everyone involved before you look for a job in a new location. Looking for a job in another place takes money and commitment. That's why it's important that you be clear about your motivation. You have to want to do this.

WHAT TO HASH OVER WHEN DECIDING
WHERE TO MOVE AND WORK

If you've moving because you want to be near your eighty-year-old father who resides in Poughkeepsie, then I guess it's pretty clear where you're moving to. But the type of work you do and how close you want to be to your father will affect where you actually end up.

Take the case of the woman who lived in Los Angeles and wanted to be near her mother in Cleveland. Since she worked in the toy industry, she moved to Cincinnati, where a toy manufacturer was headquartered and could use her skills at the time she was looking. She compromised a bit. But now, instead of being 2,053 away from her mother, she was only 245 miles away. That's a four-hour drive one way as opposed to a five-and-half-hour plane ride one way.

If you want to move to a place and job that allows for more leisure time, shorter commutes, and more flexibility, you'll look for locations and situations that give you that freedom.

Likewise, if you're moving because of your son's allergies, then that will be the main factor affecting where you end up; but there are many other things to consider. And if you're moving for a lifestyle change or your first job out of college, you have more flexibility and more factors to think about.

Of course, not all factors will be equally important to you; so create your own livability profile. This reflects the criteria that are important to your life. Here is a list of things to consider.

◆ LIVABILITY PROFILE

People in the Community

Is diversity important to you? How about average age? Are you a part of a particular religious or ethnic group? Is it important to be among people with similar interests or beliefs?

Physical Environment

Some places are urban, rural, noisy, polluted, or remote, or have lots of traffic. What appeals to you? Do you care if your proposed location is prone to tornadoes, earthquakes, or hurricanes?

Other Environment Factors

One environment might be more family-oriented than another. Some places are business-oriented, have a small-town or big-city mentality, are provincial, conservative, laid-back, entrepreneurial, or more oriented to singles. What matters to you?

Cost of Living

Taxes and costs for housing, transportation, food, and recreation will vary widely. How much does this affect you?

Commute

What kind of transportation system is important to you? Do you need a car to get around? Do you need to be close to an airport?

Health Care

How important is it to be near hospitals, clinics, or medical specialists? Do you or your family have special medical needs?

Crime Rate

What priority does this have in your life?

Education

If you have children, education and easy access to schools is probably a priority.

Social and Cultural Life

What do you enjoy doing in your free time? Do you like art exhibits, symphonies, theater, university programs, museums, good food? If you are young and single and want a lively social life, what kinds of social interaction do you want?

Recreation

What sports or other recreational activities do you enjoy?

Climate and Landscape

Some areas are hot, cold, humid, sunny, gray, windy, snowy, damp, dry, rainy. Do you like being near a desert, mountains, an ocean, lakes, grass, open spaces?

Business Climate and Economy

Some communities are in a growth mode, while others are slow and steady. What is important for your line of work? Is it important or necessary for your spouse or partner to work? Are there quality opportunities in his or her field?

Industries

What types of industries affect your career and type of work? Do you need to be near manufacturers or service industries such as banks and insurance, retail, high-tech, and universities?

Now spell out what each item in the profile means to you. Then prioritize them in order of importance *to you*. The following worksheet will help you organize your priorities.

"What's Important to Me" Worksheet

Describe what you would like in   *Prioritize it in order of importance:*
the following areas.

People in the community _____

_____

_____

Physical environment _____

_____

_____

Other environment factors _____

_____

_____

Cost of living _____

_____

_____

Commute _____

_____

_____

Crime rate _____

_____

_____

Education _____

_____

_____

Social and cultural life _____

_____

_____

Recreation _____

_____

_____

Climate and landscape _____

_____

_____

"What's Important to Me" Worksheet continued

Business climate and economy _____

_____

_____

Industries _____

_____

_____

WHERE TO GET THE LOWDOWN ABOUT PLACES

If you have a specific location in mind and want to learn what it's like to live there, there are many sources of information available—some of which I list in the Appendix. For instance, most public libraries loan videotapes that help you discover information about regions and major cities.

If you're not set on a location, there are services that can help you. A company like Location Guides will create your own personal relocation analysis. For fifty dollars, they ask you about your priorities when it comes to things like cost of living, crime rate, climate, size of city, and educational opportunities. They sort through their databases of U.S. statistics and prioritize the regions based on your input, then search for cities that meet your most important criteria.

Location Guides also publishes the *Location Report*, which has a very thorough listing of statistics for cities in every state covering: crime rate, air quality, average temperature, such environmental risks and hazards as earthquakes and tornadoes, poverty levels, acreage of recreational land, pupil/teacher ratio, high school graduation rate, AIDS cases, heart disease and cancer deaths, number of cars per road mile, and hazardous waste sites, just to mention a few.

When it comes to information about business opportunities and the economic future of an area, Location Guides lists economic and employment factors such as business growth rate, unemployment rate, average hourly earnings, employment figures, annual average employment change, number of building permits, number of businesses in the county, number of businesses, and average income statistic.

The report lists local contacts for getting more information. Location Guides (www.locationguides.com) also publishes its top-ten lists twice a year in which they grade 207 metropolitan areas in ten categories: population, climate, risks, cost of living, crime, employment, health, education, economy, and environment. Call or write them at:

P.O. Box 58506

Salt Lake City, UT 94158

Telephone: 801/645-7252.

There's a web site that lists state and local government on the net, where, if you go to a particular locale, you can look up all kinds of information: events in that city, neighborhoods, ordinances and resolutions passed by local government, public meetings, city job openings and programs such as curbside recycling (http://www.piperinfo.com/state/states.html).

Utne Reader published its list of "America's 10 Most Enlightened Towns" (one is Canadian) in its May–June 1997 issue. These are towns that "are making a special effort to foster connectedness and contentment among all the people who live in them." The article makes a point of saying that these communities "may not score that well on a traditional checklist of advantages and disadvantages." But, rather, it's a list of places that seem to deal creatively with challenges they face. In case you're interested, these towns are Ithaca, New York; Portland, Oregon; Durham, North Carolina; Burlington, Vermont; Madison, Wisconsin; Arcata, California; Portland, Maine; Iowa City, Iowa; Providence, Rhode Island, and Toronto, Canada.

Places Rated Almanac and *Money* magazine publish its online annual survey of The Best Places To Live (www.pathfinder.com/money/bestplaces/).

Based on forty-one quality-of-life factors, *Money* covers America's 300 largest metro areas. It's one of the easiest ways I have found to search all kinds of information about a specific location: job growth forecast, median price of a home, crime rate, number of library books per capita, number of four- and five-star restaurants, average commute time, average annual rainfall, snowfall, and temperatures. If you want to do a cost-of-living comparison on where you live now and where you're thinking of moving to, you can get that too.

The *ACRA Cost of Living Index*, published by the American Chamber of Commerce Researchers Association, is another source for comparing cities' costs of living. It is available at most public libraries.

But, as *Money* points out on its web site, people's preferences change and a region's fortune may shift, causing an area to move up or down in appeal from year to year.

For instance, an article in *Fortune* magazine (November 1997) entitled "North America's Most Improved Cities" reports on places that have made the greatest strides, and are therefore poised to be in the best shape to capitalize on opportunities to come. According to the magazine's investigation, many cities have diversified their economic base, strengthened their service sectors, beefed up infrastructure, and made improvements that attract business and add to the quality of life. They looked at everything from opportunities for recreation and culture to crime level, quality of schools to number of Starbucks, miles of bike paths and number of movie screens.

So you need to take all the information into consideration and take some of it with a grain of salt. In other words, just because somebody rates Fargo, North Dakota, above average in all categories or gives kudos to Fayetteville, Arkansas, for its low cost of living, strong economy, and low crime rate, neither place may be what you have in mind for your life. What one list rates as the

Most Livable City in America might not fit your definition. To some people, being five minutes from Nordstrom's is heaven. To someone else, it's being fifty miles from the nearest city. *Prioritize what's important to you.* Whose life is it anyway?

2

WHAT YOU CAN DO FROM HOME

Odds are you would like to have this process go as quickly as possible. So in case it has crossed your mind to just hop a plane, train, or any other vehicle and head straight for wherever you want to move in order to hurry things along, hold your horses. This is not smart. It's also not practical, now is it? Especially if you have a job. Even if you're not working right now, it's not only a dumb idea, but a potentially mucho expensive one.

This whole process of getting a job in another place—and it is a process—is not like ordering a Triptik from the AAA. When conducting a long-distance job search, you will need to travel sundry routes, figuratively speaking, by getting involved in different strategic activities. And be prepared to run into some obstacles. All will not be clear sailing.

The good news is you can do much of this work from the comfort of home—and you will not only be saving money, but you'll accomplish a lot more. You see, if you want to make a grand entrance and be welcomed with open arms in your target market, as well as make the most of your time and money when you do show up, you've got to prepare your landing. That will require weeks of work and preparation sitting at your computer or typewriter, on the phone, in the library, and on the Internet right in your hometown.

So let's talk about the three main activities you'll be involved in at home: (1) establishing your goal and strategy, (2) conducting research, and (3) preparing to write, call, and meet people. Now let's talk about each one in detail.

FIRST: STAKE YOUR CLAIM AND PLOT A STRATEGY

You need to be very clear about your goal; then you can decide how you're going to meet it. Is your goal to find a job in a particular city or area? Or is it to get a job in a targeted industry and it doesn't matter where the job is? Or are you open to both? It's important to decide what your goal is so you know what steps to take next.

I'll give you an example. I had a client named Sarah who was in operations management. She wanted to live in Portland, Oregon, to be closer to family. She was willing to work for any type of manufacturer where her background would be valued, so her number one goal was to find a job in operations management in Portland. But since she had been laid off, was the breadwinner for her family, and needed to find a position within six months (when their finances would be strained), she worried about whether she could achieve her goal in that time frame.

To increase her odds of finding employment quickly, Sarah also decided to consider remaining in her industry—food processing. Since there are a limited number of food processors in Portland, she expanded her search to include any area in the country. She wasn't thrilled with this option, but nevertheless felt she needed an alternative plan. Therefore, Sarah had two goals, one that she liked better than the other. With that in mind, she developed Plan A and Plan B.

Plan A supported goal one: to find a position in Portland where her operations background could be used. Everything she did while conducting Plan A supported that goal.

Now I'm jumping ahead here by telling you what she did, but it helps make my point. Sarah then:

- Created a database of the names of manufacturers in the Portland area from library directories and lists on the Internet.
- Subscribed to Portland's business paper, the *Business Journal of Portland*, and also *The Oregonian* to get acquainted with companies and the business climate there.
- Asked the Portland Chamber of Commerce to send her information on area businesses.
- Met with three people she knew in the city where she was living who used to live in Portland. They gave her names of companies (in particular, small ones that weren't so easy to find in a directory) to add to her list and names of people they knew whom Sarah could talk to later. (Later on, she wrote letters to these people and met them when she visited Portland, which I'll talk about in Chapter 3.)
- Posted her résumé on several online recruiter sites and job banks. (I will get into this later.)

About two months after implementing Plan A, Sarah put Plan B into action, which supported goal two: to find an operations management position with a food processing company anywhere in the country. And everything she did while conducting Plan B supported that goal. Sarah:

- Created a database of names of food processors across the country.
- Read the food service manufacturers association newsletter to find out what companies were growing or starting up and which operations management employees may have just gotten a new job that left an opening elsewhere.
- Attended regular meetings at the local chapter of management professionals and talked to her colleagues to find out if they were aware of any potential openings in their industry and to get their thoughts on her search.

• Called or wrote the professional trade associations in her industry to get a copy of their newsletter and, when possible, ran a "position wanted" ad in the newsletter.

• Posted her résumé on the Internet with several recruiters and job banks.

Both of her strategies included these activities:

1. Getting information
2. Writing people
3. Calling people
4. Meeting people

Do you now see why you need to be clear about your goal before you know what action to take next? It would be ideal if you could concentrate on just one goal at a time, but sometimes, like in Sarah's situation, you may not feel comfortable doing that. Many of my clients concentrate on their Plan A first—their preferred goal—and set a time limit. If they haven't achieved their goal by that date, Plan B kicks in.

You may be interested in looking for a job in two or three different *targeted* cities at the same time. This is different than Sarah's second objective—to find a job in her industry *anywhere* in the country. In other words, Sarah was targeting her industry, not a specific location. If you're looking for a job in two or three different target areas, in most circumstances I'd suggest you prioritize those areas and investigate them one at a time in *order* of priority.

For example, say you pick Washington, D.C., Boston, and Chicago as target cities. You'd start by focusing on your first priority— Washington, D.C. Once you've got activity going on there, it might make sense to start investigating your second priority. It depends on how successfully your D.C. search is going. If you're not getting very far and don't see much progress in the near future, then go to your second priority.

Beware of a potential problem that can arise when you're targeting several cities: You stretch yourself thin and have too many balls in the air. When this happens, you could begin to sound ambiguous about what you want when you talk to people.

Another strategy is to concentrate on your preferred city for a specific period of time. If you haven't made a dent there in, say, three months, or have learned that the area isn't good for your field, or find that you don't like it anymore, move on to your second priority. You can also go back and forth between strategies.

But before you do anything else, *establish your goal*, then develop a strategy or approach to meet your goal. The direction you pick will depend on the amount of time you have, your personal obligations, and your overall finances.

If you're wondering why I'm hammering you over the head with this goal and strategy thing, here's why. This whole idea of looking for a job in another place is a big endeavor. If you don't break it down into steps, it can be overwhelming and you'll probably get frustrated.

It's also easy to veer off course. That's why I not only want you to write down your goal and strategy, but also post it in the area near where you're conducting your job search—on the wall in front of you or on your desk, for instance. I want you to do this because you're going to be tempted to do things that take you off course. For instance, one day you'll be sitting there, just you and your cat, when all of the sudden an idea hits you.

"Hey," you say out loud to yourself and the cat. "Why don't I send out a thousand letters to companies all over the country and see what kind of response I get?"

If I was in the room with you, I'd say, "Now wait a minute. If your objective is to find a job in Arizona, the place you've targeted because you want to be in the Southwest and closer to your family in Nevada, why in the world would you do that?" Good point, huh?

Hey, it can happen. You could be having a really bad day, worrying about your future, feeling pressured to speed things up. So since I can't be in the room with you, please post your goal and strategy nearby. Then whenever you get an idea, look up at your goal and ask yourself, "Does this idea I just came up with support my goal?"

I'm not saying you can't change your mind once you make a plan, or that your strategy won't change as you implement your plan. Just be focused yet flexible. In other words, don't do things that have no rhyme nor reason. Here's an example of what you might post on your wall:

My goal:
To find a position in advertising in Austin, Texas.

My strategy:
 • Create a database of advertising agencies and companies that would have an advertising and marketing budget in the Austin, Texas, area from the Internet, library directories, Greater Austin Chamber of Commerce, Austin business newspapers, and purchased lists.
 • Contact people in my hometown to tell them my goal and ask for their help.
 • Attend meetings of my local chapter of the Advertising Club.
 • Write and call people I know in Austin to discuss my goal and ask for their help.
 • Meet with people in Austin that I get referred to, already know or want to talk to.

Write your goal and strategy here:

My goal: _____

_____

_____

_____

My strategy: • _____

• _____

• _____

• _____

• _____

• _____

• _____

• _____

• _____

Now that you've got your goal and strategy, let's talk more specifically about what you will do next (the first *activity* involved in your strategy of job hunting in another location and much of which you'll do in your own backyard)—conducting research.

SECOND: GET THE DIRT

The next item on the agenda is research. If that sounds unappealing, call it something else—Strategic Data That Will Help Me Get My Job, or how about Stuff I Need to Check Out. Take your pick.

What exactly are you looking for?

1. *Getting acquainted information.* This is information that will help you get acquainted with the organizations, business climate and community, and opportunities in your targeted area. No mat-

ter what your strategy, you need to know about the communities you're looking at and the types of businesses that are there.

2. *Public postings information.* This is information that will lead you to job openings in the town or city that are publicly posted. "Public posted" is a term that's used to describe a position that is listed in a variety of sources. This includes advertisements in the local newspaper, business journals, trade magazines, as well as on the Internet, and positions listed with recruiters.

Let's discuss the first type of data you need to research: *Getting acquainted information.*

In case you're thinking about skipping this step, here's one good reason you don't want to: Jobs aren't going to appear magically before your eyes; you have to dig them up. While you're getting acquainted with your targeted area, you will discover companies that you'll want to talk to, firms you don't want to talk to; you will gain insight into companies, learn what they do and their reputation. All of this will help you develop your target list. You may even uncover available jobs.

WHERE TO GET ACQUAINTED

To compile this kind of data, you're going to become a bit of a sleuth. This is where many people automatically say: "The net! The net! The net! I must get on the net! That's where I'll find everything I need to know!"

True, you will find lots of data on the Internet—more information than you know what to do with or have time to decipher, information that will take you down pathways, avenues, and alleys to other information you never dreamed anybody even thought about. But it's not the *only* source out there. (Besides, you may not have access to the Internet.)

Most of the time I have found the net to be a stupendous source of information. Other times, I can spend an hour going back and forth to fifteen different sites and come up with nothing. If you count the time it takes to find something, download it, decide whether it's worth having, then print it out, plus the times you bump the wrong key and lose your place and have to figure out where you were, or your computer crashes, research on the Internet can be extremely time consuming. It's not the answer to your research prayers.

Many of the places I suggest you go to for information *are* on the net. However, please consider other sources that can be just as beneficial in different ways. And keep in mind that much of the information now accessible through the net is also available through more traditional sources.

Before you go to the library or log on, you need to think through the kind of information you want:

♦ LISTS OF BUSINESSES IN YOUR TARGETED AREA

You can compile these through information you get online. Or you can compile them from directories and CD-ROMs at the library. Check out resources like:

• *American Business Information Directory*, a database of 10 million U.S. businesses and one million Canadian firms. You can also purchase lists from their publisher, American Business Information, at (888) 725-3753.

• *U.S. Big Business Directory*, which lists companies with 100 or more employees. They're on the net at salesleadsusa.com (so is the American Business Information Directory). You can purchase custom lists via the net or (888) 725-3753.

• *American Manufacturers Directory*, which lists over 500,000 manufacturing companies that you can search by areas like headquarters, employee size, branch locations, metro areas, and sales volume.

• *Standard & Poor's Register*, which lets you search 55,000 public and private companies by region, state, city ZIP code, area code or product. It also lists 400,000 executives and biographies of 70,000 corporate officers and directors.

If you like to wade through books, most of this information is still available in print. But CD-ROMs eliminate the hassle of pouring through cumbersome tomes, and you can customize what you're looking for on the computer. For example, let's say you want to find ad agencies. A CD-ROM lists about 31,000 nationally. Hit a key or two, you'll get a list of ad agencies in Pennsylvania. Then you can customize your search to, say, Pittsburgh, Pennsylvania.

There are more sources that I list in the Appendix—many of which you'll find in a well-stocked shelf of reference materials at your public library. Many libraries even have a special career information center nowadays. Ask the librarians for anything you don't see. They are incredibly nice and knowledgeable people and like to share information.

You can also create your database from membership directories of professional organizations, chamber of commerce member directories—even the phone book.

Check out annual best-place-to-work lists. These describe which companies have good compensation, opportunities for women to advance, child-care benefits, flexible hours, and other family-friendly perks, not to mention respect for employees. You'll find them in *Business Week* when they publish their "Best Companies for Work and Family" list, in *Fortune*'s "The 100 Best Companies to Work for in America," and *Working Mother*'s "Best Companies for Working Mothers." Some companies even go out of their way to hire couples. Take Corning, which has found it challenging to get qualified people to relocate to towns in Pennsylvania and Virginia. To make it more appealing, they try to hire spouses. How did I find out about that? By reading magazines like *Fortune*, which have stories on things like "The 100 Best Companies to Work for." That's what I mean by being a sleuth.

I have clients who want to send out a mass mailing to employers. Even though I don't necessarily recommend this, it's something they want to do. So fine, go ahead, I tell them. If you're considering buying a custom mailing list, expect to pay anywhere from fifty to a couple of thousand dollars—depending on how many names you want and in what form you want them. The smaller the volume, the more you pay for each name.

For instance, you can buy 125 mailing labels from American Business Information for fifty dollars, each name costing forty cents. The per-label price drops when you order more than 500 names. You can order lists of public and private companies based on industry, geography, ZIP code, and company size in the form of mailing labels, typed lists, 3 × 5 note cards, or a disk. Also, if you're targeting a particular organization, they will sell you a single company profile for three dollars.

In addition to general lists of businesses, American Business Information also has more targeted data, such as a list of brand-new businesses. Besides the fact that their information appears to be thorough, accurate, and up-to-date, they are very nice on the phone and will help you figure out what you need to fit your budget.

◆ READ PUBLICATIONS

These can include newspapers, trade publications, magazines, newsletters, and annual reports. Let's talk about what you can learn from them.

1. Local newspapers. They give you information about what companies are growing, expanding, or moving to your targeted area. Why do you want to know that? Well, it's likely that if a company is growing, expanding, or moving to your targeted area, jobs will follow. Sometimes a news article will come out and say just that:

Software developer R. J. Solutions, which employs 235, is expanding its Minnesota office and adding 175 jobs over the next year.

Other times, possible job leads are tucked between the lines. For example, I once found several possible job leads in the business section of a Cincinnati newspaper. The headline on one story said, "Zaring eyes Louisville." The story went on to say that this Cincinnati-based home builder is considering expansion into Louisville. If you're a professional in the building industry and want to move to Louisville, it could mean a new job.

Seem like a longshot? Just for the heck of it, I called Zaring Homes, Inc. They told me if they do expand there, that their own employees get first shot at positions such as estimators and sales, production and operations managers, but if the right person came in and said, "I'm an experienced superintendent," and they couldn't find a Zaring employee who would want to move or a qualified person there, they'd consider hiring someone from elsewhere. That's what's called being at the right place at the right time. Thing is, you need to dig around a bit to know to be there.

I once got a job by reading between the lines of a newspaper article. It said that a particular ad agency just picked up three new accounts. That could mean they'd need more staff, I thought to myself. Sure enough, when I called the creative director, they were hiring.

"How did you know we needed someone?" he asked me at our first interview. When I told him, he thought I was pretty smart.

You can also put two and two together by reading the part of the newspaper (usually in the business section) that lists the names of people who recently took a new job. It gives their new title and company, and many times the organization they just left. Guess what that means? Their old job might be available.

Even if their line of work isn't the same as yours, if they worked for a company that's in your industry and targeted area, it's another way to build your list of businesses.

On the other end of the spectrum, you can also get information on who's downsizing or just merged with another company (which doesn't necessarily mean they're not hiring; a company could be eliminating positions that aren't necessary anymore, but looking for people to fit other openings.) You can also find out who might be closing their doors.

How do you find articles about businesses in a city in which you don't live? First, you can subscribe to the local papers or read them on the net. Second, check your library.

Sources such as *Business Newsbank*, a business information resources with over 120,000 articles on companies, products, industries, and executives, collect articles on companies from local business journals, newspapers, and wire services. *Business Newsbank* can be a good source for information that's not so easy to find on small and privately held businesses. They're available at (800) 762-8182.

General Business File is an index to articles in more than 700 national business and trade publications. Many newspapers also have an archive file that you can access via the Internet.

News articles can give you clues about whom to contact when you start compiling a list of people you want to talk or write to. For instance, when one of my clients was investigating a move into a new industry as well as a new location, she dug up recent issues of the local business newspaper. One article was written by the president of a company in the industry she was targeting. She wrote to him, citing the article and some of his comments. When she called to follow up, he had forwarded her letter to his senior vice president, who set up an appointment when she visited their city later that month. She ended up getting a job offer from this company. (Much more on this whole topic of people in Chapter 3.)

2. Trade magazines. These are excellent sources for general trends in your industry. You'll find new products and services, training, books and films, information about conferences and workshops (consider attending a workshop in your area to meet people from your industry), job openings, salary surveys, insight into the kinds of problems people in the industry deal with, and people who get quoted in articles that you may want to write to.

Trade magazines are invaluable if you're conducting a national search—one like Sarah's Plan B—where you're targeting companies in a particular industry anywhere in the country.

One of my clients who was in business-to-business advertising used trade publications aggressively to find out what accounts were up for review and what advertising agencies had been invited to pitch those accounts. Having this information, he targeted the agencies who, if they got the accounts, might be adding staff to service their new account.

3. Newsletters and annual reports. Obviously you will need to have a specific company in mind when you're looking for these. So let's say you want to move to Minneapolis. You discover it's the headquarters of eighteen Fortune 500 companies, including 3M, Honeywell, General Mills, Control Data, and Land O'Lakes—all companies that you'd like to know more about.

By reading these companies' publications, you can get details on their products, sales, the faces and names of people, as well as insight into the company culture. For example, check out the stories about particular divisions and successful people in the company. What qualities do they brag about? What's important to the CEO in his or her open letter? You can get a feel for what the company and its leadership values. Just call the company's public relations or communications department for copies. I also list an online resource for annual reports in the Appendix.

◆ Research the Internet

You can get all kinds of information, including:

1. Data on companies.

There is so much available, I couldn't begin to cover it all. But to give you an idea, there are sources like Hoover's Online, which offers Hoover's Company Capsules (www.hoovers.com). This site offers information about more than 13,000 of the largest public and private companies in the U.S. and around the world. You just type in the company name or ticker symbol and you'll find the company's description, address, officers, sales and employment figures, hyperlinks to data like financial reports, stock quotes, and S.E.C. filings. Some profiles include a company's web site address.

Hoover's Online Library searches for information about a specific question you may have or for broad information on, say, the advertising industry. But if you want to view the full text of the articles you need a subscription or license to Hoover's Online, which you have to pay for.

Another place to find company profiles is at www.jobtrak. com/profiles. Companies pay $4,500 a year to be listed here, so these firms use this as a means to recruit employees. When you go to this site you'll find a brief overview of a company which links you to their web site.

I am also impressed with Thomas Register's online information (www.thomasregister.com). All you do is register (there's no cost) and you can find out about the 155,000 American and Canadian companies that are in their database. And they make it very easy for you. You search by product or service, company name or brand name. If you want details on a company's products or services, you can view an "online catalog" or order "literature by fax" and get it within minutes. You can e-mail companies on their site, and if there is something you can't find, Thomas's has a "Can't

Find It?" Information Center. By the way, their information is also available in their printed directories and on CD-ROM.

Dow Jones Interactive Publishing has a service that lets you search for news articles about your specific industry, research the performance of millions of companies, find a list of key online publications about your industry and more. They're at http://ip.dowjones.com.

There's also a source called Vault Reports that has employer profiles, information on a company's hiring process and more. The reports range in cost from $9.50 to $35. They also offer three-to four-page company summaries for $3.95 each. You can find them at 888/JOB-VAULT or http://www.vaultreports.com.

Some states now offer web sites that let you research companies. Take Kentucky, for example, which has a program for searching the state's entire database of its corporations (http://www.sos.state.ky.us/).

With the net, you can really hit the jackpot by looking up a particular company's web site. When I looked up 3M's Health Information Systems web site, I discovered their newest products, who they had just won contracts with, who was named national marketing manager, what they're doing globally, not to mention employment opportunities.

Or you can be more general in your search. Say you want to move to Austin, Texas, and you don't know much about the business community. You can visit a site like SiteNet, the electronic edition of *Site Selection Magazine* (www.siteselection.com/). When I opened up an article on Austin, Texas, I found out that Samsung Electronics plans to build a $1.3-billion computer chip plant there, and that Austin hosts more than 825 high-technology firms, including more than 200 semiconductor and semiconductor-related firms. It is the state capitol and home to the University of Texas; the national research consortia MCC and Sematec moved to Austin because of the university, which attracts research and development funds. The article quotes J. J.

Baskin, director of national business development for the Greater Austin Chamber of Commerce, who, if I were you, I'd put on my list of people I want to talk to.

Let's say your spouse, who works for Mead, just got transferred to Chillicothe, Ohio. At this same Internet site, I found information about Chillicothe's close proximity to Columbus and good highway connections to other metro areas. So if the kind of work you do is not in Chillicothe, or you want to work in a larger market, a commute is an option. The site also has information about other industries based in Chillicothe, including PPG Industries worldwide automotive replacement glass distribution center and several multinational firms, as well as small and medium-sized industries.

Another good place to get information on the net—and by mail—is any city's Economic Advisory Council or Department of Economic Development—they're called by different names around the country. These councils have data on businesses as well as all kinds of demographics. For instance, Palm Springs e-mailed me the location on the web to find out the growth rate of the population, median age, average number of sunny days (they get 330 days of sunshine annually, in case you're interested), cost of living, per-capita income, and housing costs.

If you are a minority and looking for very specific information, say on black-owned businesses, companies that have a commitment to diversity or recruiters who specialize in black executives, the Internet may be a place to check out.

For example, if you target advertising, you can come across the American Association of Advertising Agencies site (www.commercepark.com/aaaa/) which promotes its Multicultural Advertising Intern Program. Another example is the American Association of Medical Colleges, which has a minority recruitment program (www.aamc.org/meded/minority/recruit/start.htm).

The amount of information can be overwhelming. There's a web site that has sifted through library and reference resources on the web and can be helpful in cutting through the clutter. LibrarySpot (www.libraryspot.com) gives you sites for business and government information, maps and statistics, text from newspaper articles from around the world, information on professional associations, and industry publications.

2. Advice and information from colleagues in your field or people in a field you're researching. You do this through:

Chat Rooms: These are places where you can hold informal but serious "conversations," get advice and ask others for information about your career via your keyboard. You handle them like live conversations. That means you don't just barge into a discussion or monopolize a conversation. The authors of *CareerXRoads, the 1998 Directory to the 500 Best Job, Résumé and Career Management Sites on the World Wide Web* (MMC Group) urge you to learn the appropriate chat room etiquette before you join a conversation. There are also things called "emoticons," which are keyboard symbols or abbreviations you use to express emotions. (Some people think they're annoying.) For a chat room primer look up:

www.otn.net/chatroom/help.html

To find a chat room related to your career, they suggest:

www.clickit.com/bizwiz/bizwiz.htm

www.aboutwork.com

www.talkcity.com

Newsgroups: These are a network of discussion groups that have opinions and information on many subjects. You want to search for one that is related to your career. You can get a dialogue started by posting a question like: To what kinds of jobs can I apply my medical background besides a clinical setting? They differ from chat rooms, where you sometimes get instant responses, in that it could be days before people respond to your posting.

Listservs: This is basically a mailing list of a group of people who exchange e-mail about a particular subject. If you join a listserv devoted to your career field, you'll get mail on the subject and meet people. For information on how to use listservs and search for lists, check out:

www.liszt.com

www.reference.com

Keep in mind that you never know who you could be communicating with on the net. It could end up being someone from your company. So beware if you haven't yet announced that you're leaving your current position.

WHERE TO GET PUBLIC POSTING SCOOP

◆ RECRUITERS

Also known as headhunters, they usually have a pretty good idea of what's going on in a particular industry. At the same time, do not depend on recruiters to get you a position. It's not their job.

Many people get disillusioned when they don't hear back from headhunters or don't get any results. Keep in mind how these professionals work. Recruiters are not in the business of helping *you* find a job. They are not a clearinghouse for job openings. They are retained by a company to help the employer find a match for an opening they have. Most people simply don't want to understand this. Recruiters tell me they get dozens of calls from job hunters asking—many times *insisting*—to be interviewed.

There are two basic types of recruiters: (1) retainer recruiters, who are hired to find someone for a particular position or positions for a specific time period and are paid whether they find the right candidate or not; and (2) contingency firms, which get paid when their candidate is hired.

Recruiters can be one important part of your search, though. But I want to emphasize the word "one." If you have a relationship with one or two recruiters, it can pay off to send your résumé.

Who knows—at the very moment you send your résumé, they may have a client that has a position that fits you perfectly.

If you don't know any recruiters personally, check out a directory such as *The Directory of Executive Recruiters* (Kennedy Publications), which lists recruiters by industry, geography, and specialty. It also breaks down which ones work on retainer and which on contingency.

If you want to do a mass mailing to recruiters, you can also purchase labels, disks, and lists of recruiting firms and key contacts from Kennedy Publications at (800) 531-0007. For more information, they're on the web at www.kennedy/pub.com. You'll find a sample letter to send along with your résumé to recruiters in Chapter 3.

It can't hurt to send your résumé to recruiting firms that specialize in your field. That's one way a headhunter can find you when they do have a possible fit. But your résumé will most likely end up in their computer data bank and only be looked at further if your speciality is needed by one of their clients.

The other way a recruiter can find you is long before you're actually job hunting. So look at a recruiter as someone you're building a relationship with throughout your career.

Most likely you'll hear from recruiters not just when they have something for you. Some studies have shown that recruiters call baby boomer executives on average eleven times a year—five times about new job opportunities, four times to suggest candidates for jobs at their company, and twice to ask for references to other possible candidates.

One of my clients insisted on sending out a mass mailing to over two hundred recruiters. (You may have figured out by now that I'm not keen on mass mailings.) He got two calls back, which didn't pan out. To me, that's a waste of time and money.

One of my other clients did get many responses when he posted his résumé on this headhunter web site: www.HeadHunter.net. But for the most part, he adds, "They don't want to hear from you. It's better when they call you. That's when they're interested."

For example, this client had sent his résumé to a headhunter in early June. He called several times and never got a response. Then out of the blue, six months later, this headhunter called him.

"He expected me to know who he was. It had been so long since I'd written him, I couldn't remember him," he told me. "I said, 'Excuse me, when did I write you?' I was able to look up the letter by the date and pulled it right up on my computer."

So it just goes to show that sources such as headhunters may not be able to help you at the exact moment you call, but they may have something in the future. That's one of the big reasons I consider these long-term relationships.

If you are a recent college graduate, recruiters will see you differently than they would a seasoned professional. A good recruiter (one who's in it for the long haul and wants to build relationships with people) will probably spend some quality time with you. The recruiter will tell you honestly that they probably can't help you now, but a few years down the road, when you have experience and are ready to make a job change, he or she can help. So it behooves you to contact them now and to keep in contact. You should also give them a permanent address, not just your campus address, since you will have moved and they may want to locate you.

On the other hand, a recruiter from Management Recruiters International told me that he has helped new graduates who have technical degrees and work experience. In general, recruiters have most luck placing graduates who have co-op or senior project work. The demand is greater for someone with a technical background than for general management-trainee types.

◆ INTERNET SITES

I will just give you an overview here since this is a humongous subject. For more details, check with *CareerXRoads*. In general the Internet offers the following:

Career centers, company web pages, and job banks. These are places where employers and organizations list available positions. You respond to these via e-mail, fax, or regular mail—whatever the posting says to do.

An example of a job bank is the America's Job Bank (www.ajb.dni.us/), a computerized network of state employment services, which has links to all kinds of great information.

Since I'm mentioning good Internet sites, check out "Consider Relocation" (www.acinet.org/resource/relocate). It's jam packed with information such as: an index of newspapers, magazines, city guides, chamber of commerce guides, real estate links, maps, phone directories, weather reports, and education and health care directories.

I also found useful information on *The Wall Street Journal* Interactive Edition (http://careers.wsj.com). It offers—at no cost—access to jobs listed by job function, company, industry, and location.

There are also online services that you can subscribe to. For example, NETSHARE (www.netshare.com) is a site geared to senior executives and lists positions with salaries over $100,000. You can search by title, location, job function, or industry.

Résumé databases. You send your résumé to these and they collect them for employers who are their clients. If someone thinks you're a match for a particular opening, you'll hear back. I list some of these databases in the Appendix.

Professional organizations' sites. Many professional organizations have web sites that include information about membership as well as job listings. Many times you have to be a member to access the job listings.

One of my clients who is a purchasing manager checked the members-only site of the National Association of Purchasing

Managers every week. There he could search current job postings, post his résumé, edit or delete his résumé, or check out other on-line employment resources.

In a typical week when searching current job postings for Ohio, the area he was targeting, he found up to twenty jobs listed. Most listings tell the company name and location, job title and description, salary range, the contact, and how the company wants to be reached. He not only discovered positions but got interviews with several companies as well.

By the way, if you're not sure what a particular professional association might be called, check out the *National Trade & Professional Associations of the United States* (Columbia Books). Or try contacting the Professional Convention Management Association at www.pcma.org/ or the International Association of Conference Centers at www.iacconline.com/.

If you are a member of your college alumni association, check to see whether they have a web site that lists positions as well.

I want to add that online recruiting is still in its infancy. And it's still high-tech companies that use it the most. It's a growing trend, but research shows that it's not widely used—yet.

Newspapers. Most daily newspapers list their classified ads on the web.

For a list of specific sites that are catalogued by region, industry, and discipline, check *CareerXRoads*.

There are also sites that offer not only posted positions, but other information such as career advice and job-hunting tips. Once you register, some send you e-mail whenever your ideal job pops up in the database. You can also post your résumé or create it, then apply right online.

Now let's talk about the next activity you'll be doing from home: preparing to make connections with people.

THIRD: PAVE THE WAY TO WRITE, CALL,
AND MEET PEOPLE

People will be the key component of your job search. How else are you going to find out who's planning to leave a job, who got fired, who's going to get fired or transferred, or where a job might be created? Most of the time, those kinds of openings are never officially announced or advertised (through the kinds of public postings we just discussed). Or by the time they are, everybody and his brother is applying for them. But people in the company, or their friends and colleagues they talk to, have the most up-to-the-minute news of who's who and what's what. It's called the grapevine. So a large part of this process will involve you talking on the phone with people and meeting them face-to-face.

People are also some of your best sources of information about specific communities and the businesses there—which is what you're concentrating on now. They need to be handled with great delicacy. People will only be helpful and open to you if you treat them right. That's why we're going to spend the next few pages talking about how to pave the best route to connect with them. (In the next chapter, we'll discuss the substance of your calls and letters.) Let's start by talking about how people like to be treated.

◆ How People Like to Be Treated

Respect their time

Most people today plan where they will be, what they will be doing and with whom over the next couple days and weeks, even months. That's one reason you see so many people walking around with Franklin Planners strapped to their bodies.

They've got their prioritized daily task list, appointment schedule, telephone meetings, and personal commitments. Plus, if they follow the Franklin rules of How to Maximize Your Time, they have learned how to say "no," to avoid overcommitment and not to overschedule. So when you're trying to get information from people (and in some cases meet them) it's not very wise to start calling up a bunch of strangers and babble on about your situation and ask about their company and community. If you even get through to anyone, your reception will be, well, rather cool.

It's doubtful they'll say, "Sure I've got a half hour right now to shoot the breeze." Would you?

Let them get to know you

If someone doesn't know you, the odds of them helping you by giving you free advice and information are slim. It's not that people don't give a hill of beans about you and don't want to be helpful, but, as we just discussed, most people are busy with their own lives. They're overloaded, in fact. I get more mail from readers of my newspaper column on this subject than any other. People complain that they're doing the work of two people and that management's expectations are so high that they are required to work longer hours. Why would they drop everything to help you, someone they don't know from Adam?

People are much more receptive when, at the very least, they know you, better yet, when they like and trust you. You have none of that going for you at this point.

So my point is you need to respect people's time and give them the chance to know you. You see, if people know you and trust you, they probably won't blow you off. They'll be more willing to take time out of their busy lives to fit you in. So your goal now is to build sincere relationships with people so they will know you, like you, and want to help you.

◆ SOME CALL THIS NETWORKING

Not me. I call it building sincere relationships. Networking has gotten such a bad rap from the thousands of people who don't respect people's time and don't get to know people before asking for a favor. I refrain from using that word so I don't get misunderstood. Just for the record, let me explain the difference between building sincere relationships and "networking."

Most people think networking is what you do when you're in trouble or need something. They think it's calling up people—some of whom they haven't talked to in three years—and saying:

"Hey, Fred, how ya doing? Long time no see. Look, I'm going to be job hunting in Kansas City and I wondered if you knew anybody there I could talk to."

Or calling people they've never met in their life and saying:

"Hello, Fred, my name is Max Sununu and Lula May Johnson gave me your name because she thought you could give me some advice on how to look for a job in Kansas City."

That's just downright rude. Not to mention stupid. Why would Fred give Max the time of day?

Some people think networking is calling up people and holding phony-baloney conversations. Take the call a client of mine got from a woman she hadn't talked to in years. This woman starts off telling my client how much she likes her company. Then she asks a lot of questions about her life. Of course, my client is suspicious. What's with this woman's sudden renewed interest? When she asked this woman the purpose of her call, she gets to the heart of it. The woman had just gotten a new job as a salesperson and wanted my client to refer her new business. Is she going to do that? What do you think? Nothing doing.

Others think networking is that thing they do at breakfast meetings where a hundred or so businesspeople gather to hear a speaker. Before the speaker gives his or her presentation, someone announces it's time to "network," and for the next five minutes everyone scatters around the room shoving their business cards into as many hands as they can.

Those are examples of what most people do—which is going on the hunt for people who can be *useful* to their career. That's insincere.

If you're smart, you've been building sincere relationships your whole life. In a sincere relationship you have some kind of mutual interest with someone, keep in regular contact, and help each other out if you can and because you want to. You don't have to be pen pals or bosom buddies or even live in the same city. Establishing these relationships is not underhanded or insincere. It's how smart people progress in the world.

By the way, if you haven't been cultivating these kinds of relationships, I'd suggest you start now.

Assuming you have already been building relationships or want to start, here's the next step.

◆ MAKE A LIST OF:

1. *People you want to talk to in the place where you live now.*

Why in the world would you talk to people in your hometown of say, San Jose, California, if you want to move to Seattle? There are two main reasons.

Do you remember why you're talking to people in the first place? It's part of your *research* in order to get acquainted with the organizations, business climate and community, and opportunities in your targeted area.

Believe it or not, people in San Jose may have: (a) lived in Seattle or (b) know people in Seattle, even if they've never lived there. Just think about all the cities where you know people.

So if you start by talking to people who know you, like you, and want to help you, they may be able to acquaint you with organizations, the business climate and community, and opportunities in Seattle, and/or refer you to people in Seattle who will be likely to talk to you because you've been referred by someone they know and like. And people who are there know other people who work, know who's planning to leave a job, who got fired, who's going to get fired or transferred, or where a job might be created. See how that works?

It also can't hurt to talk to people who have moved to your hometown from elsewhere, people who you may or may not know. Some neighborhoods are fairly transitory. A relocated employee or spouse could have some tips for you on your overall job search.

Who specifically would you talk to?

People whose opinions you trust and you have a relationship with

This might be a friend, coworker, neighbor, colleague, former coworker or boss, relative, clergy person, college professor, or a professional you do business with, such as an attorney or doctor. My chiropractor is one of the best sources of information. He not only knows hundreds of people, but because he talks to his patients about their lives and lifestyle, he knows who's doing what. I not only found my financial planner through him, but several of my clients found me through him.

Start your list:

Name	How I know him/her	What info I hope to gain

People at professional meetings you attend

If you haven't been attending any meetings, start. These are groups like Women in Communication, American Society of Engineers, Purchasing Managers Association—you get the idea. What better place to get the most up-to-date news on what companies are doing, what it's like to work for so-and-so, who just left their job, who's got an opening, who's going to be hiring, and who knows somebody in San Francisco where you're going to be moving?

Create a list of people you meet:

_____   _____   _____
_____   _____   _____
_____   _____   _____
_____   _____   _____

People at job focus groups

People who are either unemployed or may be job hunting soon meet regularly as a support group. The group is usually affiliated with a church or nonprofit organization. Groups like this offer seminars on job-hunting skills and develop relationships with employers in the city. This is another place to meet new people and build sincere relationships. And who knows? Someone may even know companies in your industry, your targeted market or people who live there.

Write down people you meet:

_____   _____   _____
_____   _____   _____
_____   _____   _____
_____   _____   _____

2. *People you already know in your targeted area.*

Many of my clients have targeted a particular area because they have friends or family they know there. So if you know people in your targeted area, by all means, you'll want to talk to them.

Name	How I know him/her	What I hope to gain
_____	_____	_____
_____	_____	_____
_____	_____	_____
_____	_____	_____
_____	_____	_____
_____	_____	_____

3. *People you want to meet*

While you're conducting your research you may read about someone in an article who you'd like to talk to in order to find out more about his or her industry and, specifically, how this company is growing over the next few years. In that case, remember, you're not approaching the person for a job. You don't even know if he or she has one for you. So don't put on any pressure. You're contacting the person to get to know him or her, learn about the area, the industry, the company, and, perhaps, just maybe, the contact will be willing to tell you who might be hiring.

Then, again, you may know a lot about a company and want to express your interest in working there. I had a client who wanted to work for Dell Computers. When she was preparing her job search, she found the right manager to contact and sent him a letter telling him of her interest.

In the next chapter, I'll show you the kinds of letters you can write to such people and what you can accomplish in face-to-face meetings.

For now, I want you to see how you can begin connecting with people while you're in your hometown. Ultimately, they will help you get to people in the place you want to move to.

Name of person I'd like to meet	Title/ Company	How I found him or her	What I hope to gain
_____	_____	_____	_____
_____	_____	_____	_____
_____	_____	_____	_____
_____	_____	_____	_____
_____	_____	_____	_____
_____	_____	_____	_____

♦ NO SHORTCUTS

So far, we've talked about the three things you need to do from home:

1. Establish your goal and develop an overall strategy.
2. Get information.
3. Prepare to write, call and talk to people.

You have to do it all. I've probably said enough about why you need to set a goal and develop an overall strategy. So let me harp once more on why you *have* to gather as much information as you can and prepare yourself to connect with people.

Both activities will help you get acquainted with the organizations, business climate, and opportunities in your targeted area and dig up posted jobs. As you're researching information, you'll end up talking to people. And as you're talking to people, you'll uncover even more information. Even though I've spelled them out as separate activities, you'll find that they overlap and feed on each other.

And while I'm on the subject of gathering information, let me stress that you need to gather *both* kinds—*getting acquainted data* and *public postings*. I know it's tempting to just put your résumé in an electronic résumé bank, check out job postings, or answer ads from the newspaper. But don't spend all your time on it.

Way before I came along, many very educated people went to great lengths to find out how jobs were discovered. They conducted surveys and research and concluded that most jobs are "found" by:

- Putting pieces of information together about who's who, who does what, who owns what, and who's got big plans for the future
- Initiating contact with people and asking intelligent questions about businesses, business trends, and areas of growth
- Applying information you discover through people and following up with them and new acquaintances
- Meeting a business owner or manager who has a problem that you can solve
- Talking to someone at a company who knows of a position that will be open but hasn't been announced yet

In other words, the majority of the better jobs are found or created by knowing current events and decision makers in an area, through strategic and planned discussions with people and by presenting yourself as a valuable professional when you go to talk to people. Based on my personal experience and that of thousands of other job hunters, I concur.

When people hear this logic, they either:

1. Agree wholeheartedly and go out and do everything they can in order to find out current trends and the status of particular businesses, then plan and hold strategic discussions with people.
Or
2. Politely listen and tell me how good that sounds. Next they explain how they think it's much smarter to just go straight to the known openings by checking out a company's job postings

on a web site or career center or answering ads from the newspaper. And then they go and only do that.

I admit, it may *seem* smart to spend all your time just going for the known openings. But here are four reasons why it's not:

1. Most jobs—the really good jobs—aren't listed *anywhere*. *Some* will be in job banks, in the newspaper, or listed with headhunters, but most will not.

2. You are one of hundreds or more job hunters responding to the posted opening. Most everybody else is thinking like you, so your chances of finding a job by waiting for a company to find you or for you to find an advertised position that fits you are slim.

3. By only responding to posted positions, you have very little control over your job search. Think about it. You respond by sending your résumé and cover letter (sometimes to companies that don't even list their names). Then you wait and see what happens. And you wait. Maybe they call you back. Maybe they don't. Not much you can do, is there?

4. By only responding to posted positions, you're basically saying you're willing to take what you can get. You need to be better acquainted with your targeted area to know the other possibilities, to potentially create a new position and get what you really want.

So, if you want to:

- Find the majority of jobs that aren't and won't be listed in any type of advertisement
- Get a jump on the hundreds of other job hunters who will be responding to an open position before it's advertised
- Be in the advantageous position of knowing who will be hiring and could use your skills
- Be in the enviable position of creating a job for yourself
- Be in control of your job search

... then you need to not only find public postings, but also get acquainted with the organizations, business climate and community and opportunities in your targeted area.

YOU MEAN I HAVE TO TALK TO PEOPLE?

By now you have gotten the message loud and clear that you will be out there in the world talking to people—some of them total strangers. This may be, shall I say, uncomfortable for you?

Some people feel as if they're bothering people. Others are just anxious or shy about talking to people—which I found to be a big problem for many.

A man once wrote me: "Being a shy person, I realize this is the biggest obstacle I face when I'm forced to meet new people. Do you have special tips for us shy people? Shy people will not listen to extroverted people who believe going out and talking to people is easy and normal behavior."

Making overtures to new people makes a lot of people nervous. Even the most outgoing person can feel as if he is thrusting himself on people who don't want to be bothered. That's all the more reason why you need to build natural alliances, starting with people you know.

But for the shy and very nervous, here are some tips:

• Get rid of the labels "normal" and "abnormal" behavior. So you don't like to initiate meetings with strangers. You're not bad, abnormal, or weak. Think of it like this: You love to work in your garden and your neighbor would rather go to Arthur Murray dance classes. Is something wrong with either you or your neighbor? No. You just have different preferences.

• Understand that this is who you are and that you're more comfortable with the inner world of ideas and things.

• Explore whether you're truly shy or just anxious. Psychologist Meredith Reid describes shyness as temperament. "Shy people may not like social stimulation or enjoy people coming at them," she says. Most people are more likely anxious. They anticipate that negative things are going to happen or situations will go badly—one of the biggest reasons people don't try to do things. Gradually expose yourself to situations you don't feel you do well in, says Reid. "You'll have some successes and be able to say, 'That wasn't so bad.' "

• Lower your expectations. Don't expect to go into a meeting with someone and be outgoing and smooth as silk. Change your definition of success to something more realistic. Expect to shake someone's hand, look her in the eye, and hold a productive conversation.

• If you are a shy person, acknowledge your strengths. Shy people are quiet people who are often good listeners, says Reid. Have a few points you want to get across in a meeting and concentrate on those. Practice what you want to say.

• Look at this activity of talking to people differently. Instead of being "forced to meet new people," see it as a really smart and pragmatic way to get what you want in your career.

Now let's talk about how you'll contact these people and what you'll say when they pick up the phone or you're eyeball to eyeball.

3

LINE UP YOUR CHEERLEADERS

All that information I just told you to gather is useless—unless you know how to use it wisely. So that's what I'm going to tell you how to do next. No point in beating around the bush.

Now when I say "use it wisely" I mean to think through strategically what you want and the best way to get it. Remember, you now have:

- Your goal and strategy that you were supposed to post on the wall
- All that initial research (getting acquainted and public postings information)
- The lists you created of people you want to talk to

You're going to use all of that to implement the next two steps—writing and calling people. But first, some strategic thinking and planning. Here are four things you must do before you write a letter or pick up the telephone:

1. Think about what you want from people
2. Consider how people will react to you
3. Understand what people will want to know about you
4. Plan what you'll say about yourself

Let's walk through each of these items.

1. ASK YOURSELF: WHAT DO I WANT FROM PEOPLE?

If you're thinking, "Well, that's simple. I want them to help me get a job"—you're not thinking strategically. Yès, a new job in your targeted market will be the end result, but you will get there by building bridges. This is what people can help you do. If you go into this believing people will help you get a job just because you ask for it, you're going to take a real beating.

So let's try again. You want people to:

- Get to know you, like you, and want to help you
- Understand your objective and become a cheerleader for you
- Help you by sharing information, ideas, and referrals to people they know, which can ultimately lead to the discovery of your next position

Each person will have different types of information to share, so you'll also need to think about specific questions to ask each person (which does not include asking if they know of any jobs for you).

If you ask people if they know of any jobs, 99.9 percent of the time, they'll sigh, look up to the sky, think about if for about ten seconds, then say, "Nope, sorry." Then they feel badly because they couldn't help and you feel badly because you feel as if you made them feel badly. Plus you didn't get anywhere.

So ask people for something they can give you so everyone is happy. That would be information about growing businesses, ideas about who's doing what, referrals to other people, and feedback on how you come across.

Sometimes job hunters who are generally suspicious and cynical say to me: "This is just an underhanded way to get contacts." There's nothing underhanded about it at all. You're not going to people for a list of their so-called contacts. What good would that do? You're certainly not asking them for a job. See how far that gets you.

No, you're being forthright and honest. You're telling people your situation and asking for their input and referrals to others they know who might be able to give you useful feedback. Along the way, if you talk to enough people and present yourself well, odds are somebody is going to know somebody who is hiring.

2. THINK: MMMM, HOW WILL THEY REACT?

When you tell someone you're looking for a job, say, in San Francisco, you're going to get a reaction. What kind will depend on who the people are and how happy they are with their own life. Let's look at the various people you might talk to and how they could react to you.

◆ PEOPLE WHERE YOU LIVE NOW

Remember, these can be folks you used to work for or with, neighbors, friends, relatives, other professionals, or college professors—anyone whose opinion you respect.

People who are secure with themselves and genuinely care about your welfare will say things like: "Really? That's exciting! I love San Francisco." Then they'll ask questions about why you have decided to move there, whether you know anyone there, and so on. They may also exhibit sadness because they genuinely like you and don't want you to leave. These people will probably want to be instrumental in helping as much as they can. They are wonderful to have on your side. Bless them.

People who are not so secure and wish they had the nerve to make a change, will say things like: "San Francisco? Why would you want to move there? They have earthquakes. The cost of living is ridiculous. You can't buy property there, it's one of the most expensive places in the whole country. Who do you know there? It's so far away."

It is unproductive to spend time with people like this. So don't.

Resist the urge to contact someone you haven't talked to in years because you know they used to live in San Francisco. If you do contact them, they might be aloof. Can you blame them? The way they see it, you haven't given two hoots about them all these years. Now the only reason you care is because you need them. I would suggest you stick with people you have stayed connected to.

◆ PEOPLE WHO LIVE IN YOUR TARGETED AREA

People in that community (not necessarily employers) might be pleased as punch that you want to live there. Others will be skeptical. What are you trying to get away from? Why do you want to move here?

Employers will be curious about your commitment level. From their point of view, you've got one big strike against you. You don't live there. That means (1) you could cost them more money than someone who's right there in town and (2) you may not be committed.

Not fair? you say. Fair, shmair. Only reality counts. If you're smart, you'll use this to your advantage by anticipating the employer's point of view (and people who may be referring you to employers) by being prepared to overcome any objections.

So you've got to consider how people will react in order to decide whether you even want to talk to them. And you need to think through how you'll be perceived in order to position and package yourself the right way. This is what we'll get into next.

What's This Positioning Stuff Anyway?

Positioning is a term coined by communications consultant Jack Trout to describe, not what you do to a product, but what you do to the mind. For example, when President Bill Clinton (the product) first ran for office, he wanted to change the public's perception of Democrats as the liberal party. So he tried to position himself in our minds as the "New Democrat." He carried out this positioning by weaving conservative issues such as welfare reform and the need to reduce the budget deficit into his campaign.

In this case, you're the product. And the minds you want to do something to are those of the people you'll be talking to. You want them to see you in a certain way.

For instance, you may want them to see you as a strong manager with a track record in production, packaging, and inventory control known for your ability to solve technical problems and personnel issues. But you also want them to see you as someone who's committed to moving to your target area and with good reason.

You'll need to influence them with simple, well-planned language and weave in information that supports how you want to be seen. So keep in mind the things already on their mind that you need to influence.

3. YOU'VE GOT THREE THINGS TO EXPLAIN

Whether you're talking to people you know, potential employers or people you get referred to, there are three things that most everyone will want to know:

1. Who you are (if they don't know you)?
2. Why do you want to move?
3. How committed are you to making this move?

Of course, employers are going to want to know more details about your background and how you'll contribute to their company and much more. We'll get into that further in Chapters 4 and 5. For now, let's concentrate on the key information you need to be prepared to present in order to position yourself during your *initial* contact with people.

4. MAKE IT SHORT AND SWEET

People have short attention spans, and unless you are clear and to the point, their minds will wander. They will also judge you from the first word you utter. If you sound uneasy and unsure of yourself, it reflects on your professional ability. This means you have to come up with a brief and concise explanation of the three things that people will want to know. From this point on, let's refer to this brief explanation as your "Move Mantra."

◆ SAMPLE "MOVE MANTRAS"

For a seasoned professional:

(Why you're looking to move and how committed you are):
"I have worked for Jones & Jeremy Co. for eight years. We were just bought out by a competitor and they are closing our offices on the West Coast and laying off the staff. I'm disappointed because I've enjoyed working here and had planned on staying for several more years. However, now I'm looking at this as an opportunity to move back to the Midwest where my parents live. My husband and I have two children and would like them to be able to see their grandparents more often. I've very committed to moving there and plan to be in a new position within six months. I've already contacted a realtor there."

(Your objective and career overview):
"My objective is to find a position in the Indiana area where I can contribute my extensive experience in operations management. I have a fourteen-year track record in leading complex organizations in the telecommunications industry through change and overseeing day-to-day operations, strategic planning and developing a team structure."

For a recent graduate:

(Why you're looking to move and how committed you are):
"I recently graduated from the University of San Diego School of Law and am a member of the California Bar. I not only went to school there, but also worked as a research assistant for a law professor and was a legal assistant at an international law firm in the area. This past summer I was a judicial extern for a judge. I have some family here, have grown attached to the area, and now I'd like to make it my home.

(Your objective):

"My objective is to find a position in the San Diego area where I can contribute my academic experience, comprehensive knowledge of corporate tax law, exposure to international taxation, and hands-on practical experience to a law firm."

This is one of the most useful exercises you can go through in a long-distance job search because you will be in so many situations where you're asked these exact questions. You'll use a version of this in just about every conversation you have and letter you write. So make it easy on yourself and come up with the general wording to answer the three main questions everyone's going to want to know: Who are you, why do you want to move, and how committed are you to the move? Know it so well, you can recite it in your sleep.

By creating these statements, right off the bat you position yourself the way *you* want the rest of the world to see you. You don't have to go on the defensive. You present the logic behind your desire and commitment to move before you're even asked. Or you're prepared when you are asked. You'll come across as clear on what you want and why, and bound and determined to get it. You start building trust. People will be more apt to take time to help you. They'll know you're serious.

If you don't think this through, you're going to end up saying something like:

"I need to move because I got laid off. This giant conglomerate swallowed up our company and didn't give a darn about us and just closed us down. Now I'm in a real bad situation. I'd like to be closer to our folks back in Indiana, so this seems like as good a time as any to do it."

You sure don't sound like someone I'd want to know, let alone burden my friends and associates with.

Or:

"I just graduated with a degree in Business. My parents live in the middle of nowhere here in Oklahoma—I'd never get a job that pays well around here. So I want to move to a big city where I can live on my own, get some good experience, and have a decent social life."

◆ WHEN TO USE YOUR MOVE MANTRA

Here are the situations in which you'll present a part of or your entire Move Mantra:

1. On the phone with people you're going to talk to in your hometown
2. In meetings with people you know in your hometown
3. On the phone and in letters to people you know, get referred to, and want to meet in your target area
4. In meetings with people in your target area

Don't worry about sounding like a broken record. Each time you talk to someone, remind yourself that this person has never heard this information. He or she, just like the last person, wants to know who you are, why you want to move, and how committed you are to moving. And even if you mentioned your situation in your letter or they heard about it through someone else, assume they forgot. They probably did.

YOU'RE READY TO CALL, WRITE, AND MEET

Remember, you're building a giant bridge to where you want to be—through people, and how you position yourself with these people. They can be a source of information about your targeted area that you can't find in a book or on the net. And they can refer you to people you don't yet know—some of them hotshot decision makers. These are going to be some of your key contacts as you plan visits to your targeted area. So here's how to start lining up your cheerleaders.

◆ 1. CALL YOUR LIST OF "PEOPLE IN THE CITY WHERE I LIVE"

Your Objective

To get them to meet with you so you can:

- Help them understand your career objective, rationale, and commitment to moving
- Get their input on your strategy, what the area you're considering is like, and specific businesses, plus referrals to individuals they may know there

How many meetings should you have? That depends. How many people do you know who can give useful advice or can tell you what the area is like, and offer referrals to individuals they may know there?

If you're moving to Parkville, Missouri, where no one you

know knows a soul, still try to set up meetings with people where you now live. Ask people whose opinions you respect for input on the best way to find a job in another place if they've done it. Ask for general advice on job hunting or for feedback on what you'll be telling people when you start interviewing.

These people may know someone in town who has actually lived in your target market or done business there and therefore can refer you to them. You'll get to practice your Move Mantra and you could end up with some good advice as well.

By the way, if you're employed and looking for a job in another location, you may be wondering if you should talk to people you work with. That can be touchy. Unless you are super-close friends with someone whom you trust implicitly, don't tell colleagues at work. If you do spill the beans with coworkers you're not ex-tremely chummy with, be prepared for the word to get out.

If you're a spouse or partner of someone who's moving for a job, and *you're* the one job hunting, you too need to be sensitive to this issue. Think through when it's the right time to tell your boss and coworkers that your partner is moving and, guess what—so are you. You don't want to be without a job before you're ready.

What to Say on the Phone

"Hi, Nan, this is Morry. How did your yard sale go? How are the kids?" (Build rapport.)

"The reason I'm calling is that I'd like to get your input." (Get to the point; she doesn't have all day.)

"You know I've been thinking about making a move to the West Coast for years. Well, they're closing our facility here. So Janet and I think the time is right to head West and we are investigating a move to San Diego." (Give her a chance to say "Wow, really?" and other expletives.)

"Since you lived there for a few years and still have relatives there, I was wondering if you'd mind sitting down with me to talk about the business climate and the area in general . . ." (pause for her response). "Great. How does this Thursday night look?"

Unless the person doesn't know anything about your situation and you need to fill in more details, wait until you meet to elaborate.

What if someone says, "I don't think I can help"? Explain to them again why you think they'd be helpful. If you trust their judgment and just want feedback on your Move Mantra, say that. (Of course, they won't know what your Move Mantra is. Just say you want feedback on what you'll be telling people during your job search.) Assure them that they've been helpful to you in the past and you have some specific advice you'd like to get from them.

◆ 2. MEET WITH THESE PEOPLE

For the most part, these are casual meetings you set up in their home or over a drink or meal out somewhere. (You spring for it.) But don't let the casual nature of the setting or your relationship dictate the agenda. Otherwise you could end up chit chatting the time away.

Your Objective

To help them understand:

- Your career objective, rationale and commitment to moving
  and

To get their input on:

- What your targeted area is like
- What the general business climate is like (if they know)

- Specific businesses and referrals to individuals they may know there
- How you present yourself
- Long-distance job-hunting techniques

Go to your meeting with specific questions each person can answer best.

If you're talking with someone who doesn't know your target area, but you want general advice and feedback, your objective is to find out how they were successful in finding a job in another location and/or how they think you will be perceived. Share your Move Mantra, explain your strategy, and ask for ideas on obstacles you might face and how to overcome them. Everyone's got an opinion.

What to Say in Your Meeting

"Thank you again for meeting with me, Nan. I know you've been really busy with your kids' new school, so I appreciate you taking time out." (Establish rapport and thank her for her time.)

"As I mentioned on the phone, we've decided to finally make the move we've talked about for years. With the business closing, the timing is right. So Janet and I are both going to look for jobs in San Diego and our plan is to be there by the end of the year.

"Since you lived there, I thought you'd be a great person to talk to for input on everything from neighborhoods to the types of businesses there." (Restate your goal and purpose of your meeting. Even if she remembers, she's had two hundred things on her mind since you first mentioned it. This will help focus the conversation.)

"I'm doing a lot of research through the Internet and the library, writing to the Chamber of Commerce and all that, but you have a good sense of overall trends and were so involved in the community there, I'd really like to get your insights.

"I know we've been neighbors for a long time and it's not like we're strangers, but I'd like to give you an overview of my work and what I'm hoping to do there." (As neighbors, the only things you may have ever chatted about is lawn care, speeding cars on your street, assessment taxes, and baby-sitters.)

"I have worked for First and Foremost Inc. for nine years as vice president of operations. I probably would have stayed for several more years if we hadn't been bought out.

"My objective is to find a position in the area where I can use my extensive experience in operations management and customer service. I have an eighteen-year track record in leading complex organizations in the financial services industry through change and overseeing day-to-day operations and strategic planning. I'd like to work for another financial institution, perhaps a smaller one. The most important thing is to be with a progressive organization, one that doesn't just pay lip service to diversity and open communications. Some of the things I'm most proud of in my position here is having created a work environment that resulted in the highest rated employee satisfaction surveys in the entire company. We did that by having a commitment from senior management to changing the corporate culture.

"So with that background, I have a few questions . . ."

Most likely you're not going to just spew out all that information at once. Take a breath. Let your neighbor, or whoever it is you're talking to, comment or ask questions. Remember, this is a conversation with an objective. Take notes. She may say something that makes you think of something else. Go with the flow.

Share what you've learned in your research. Ask her questions you haven't been able to get answered. Ask about specific companies you're interested in. I tell my clients to go in with a typed list of companies they've researched and show it to people. It's a great way to spark an idea or a thought about someone they had forgotten. If you found an article on a company that grabbed your fancy, show her that. Ask about neighboring communities you may not be familiar with.

If she offers referrals to people in the course of the conversation, ask about the person. How does she know them? Why would he or she be good to talk to? This will help you decide whether you even want to contact them. And, if you do, you can build rapport and establish a better connection if you know their relationship, anticipate objections, and figure out what questions to ask. If she can't give you much input on the person, you can always try researching them on the net.

If she hasn't offered any referrals, ask her if she knows any people you should talk to when you go there to investigate further (we get to that part of your strategy in Chapters 4 and 5). Asking for referrals, however, is not the first thing out of your mouth.

By the way, when you get a referral, ask if it's okay to use her name as the person who referred you. Clarify the context in which you can use her name. For instance, if you know each other from your Women Trying to Get Pregnant Class, your referral may not appreciate you bringing this up.

At the end of the conversation, tell her you'll keep her updated—and do. She's got a vested interest in you now. People like to know how things turn out. She might be able to help more. Now that she knows what you're up to, she might get some great idea one morning in the shower, but it could slip her mind since you've never followed up. Your job search is not her responsibility. People are busy with their own lives. Besides, you could run into an obstacle later on she can help with. Keep the relationship going so you will feel okay about contacting her later if you need to.

When you get home, write a thank-you note. I don't care how well you know this person or if you do live next door. They've taken time out of their busy life to help you. That's the least you can do.

After your meeting, update your target list with data you get from these people. Research the companies.

One more thing, be open to having a meeting on the fly. You may be sitting next to someone at a dinner of your professional association one evening who has all kinds of help to offer. Take it. Be spontaneous. Every meeting doesn't have to be a planned event. This is another reason to have your Move Mantra in the forefront of your brain.

◆ 3. Call and Write People You Know in Your Target Area, Get Referred to, or Heard About and Want to Meet

Now that you've met with people in your hometown, you've got a more in-depth view of your target area, perhaps a more extensive list of companies, and hopefully some referrals to key decision makers and others in the community. You've also got the list of People You Already Know in Your Targeted Area that you compiled in Chapter 2. And if you've been researching public posting information, you might also be ready to set up interviews. (More on that in a minute.) Your research also may have uncovered someone whom you'd like to meet. Now you're ready to plan your first visit to your targeted area.

Look at your calendar and pick a period of time (up to two weeks if you can) in which you're going to visit your targeted area. TWO WEEKS?!!! Yes, that's what I'd *like* you to do. That would be ideal.

I realize that might not be convenient. You may have a job you can't leave for that long. Or family commitments. Fine. Go for as long as you can. But two weeks are optimum. Think about it. Your first round of meetings in your target area is with new people or old acquaintances. These people will refer you to people they know. So as soon as you get a referral, you have to get on the phone and set up a meeting. (I cover this fully in Chapters 4 and 5.)

You'll need at least a week to do a thorough job of meeting your first group of people, then following up with referrals they give you and setting up appointments. You might even be meeting with people the second group refers you to or have interviews with companies. But if you only have a week, accomplish as much as you can. You can still get a lot done.

Once you've picked a date, contact: (1) people you already know in your target area, (2) people you've been referred to in your targeted area, (3) people you want to interview with for an advertised position or one you discovered through someone, and (4) people you've read about and want to meet.

When contacting this fourth group, you can approach them with the intention of getting information or investigating a job with their company. It makes sense to do the latter if you know they are a start-up company, are growing, or are entrepreneurial, or if you know a lot about its structure and think it's a company where you want to work. More details on that later in this chapter.

Let's get into how to contact people in each of these groups. At the end of this chapter you'll find sample letters to send to: people you met with in your hometown who you want to thank, people you've been referred to and want to meet, companies with advertised positions, recruiters and people you've read about and want to meet.

◆ HOW TO CONNECT

I'm a big fan of letter writing. I know it's a lot easier to just pick up the phone or send e-mail. That's one of the reasons I like writing a letter, licking a stamp and finding a mailbox to stick it in. When you take time to write, you think more about what you want to say. It also sends a message to the receiver that you're serious. It's more personal. Plus, your objective is in writing. This helps position you the way you want and lessens the chance for misunderstanding. You're being a good communicator.

That doesn't mean you have to write letters to everybody. Call people you know well. Write people you haven't seen in a while or never met.

Tip: You know how rare it is that you reach someone the first time you call? Well, you'll find the same thing in this situation. After you write someone, and call back and leave a message, say three times, and you still don't hear back, you can drop another note. Explain your interest in wanting to meet. If you don't get a response after that, you probably won't get one. So don't be a pest. And don't write a letter like this one:

Dear Mr. Turnip:

Several weeks ago I wrote you to request a meeting. I was referred to you by Fanny Frazzle. I have called and left three messages and have never heard back from you. I realize you are busy, but are you so busy for even a ten-minute phone call? I am only asking for a few minutes of your time to ask you about your business. I am calling for your help, not to ask you for anything else, so I would appreciate you calling me back. Thanks for your time.

Sincerely,

Sherry Canary

The sender of this letter is from another planet if she thinks she's going to get this person's help now. By the way, this is a real letter—and I've seen worse. Writing a letter like this one is a good way to get on someone's get-lost list. There's no need to get sassy. If you're not getting the responses you want, find a new tactic—one that won't insult people.

◆ CONTACTING FOLKS YOU KNOW OR NEVER MET

Your Objective

- To introduce yourself if you've never met
- To inform them of your overall objective to find a job there and your immediate objective to visit and meet with them
- If you're writing, to prepare them for your follow-up phone call to set a meeting
- If you're calling, to set up a meeting during your visit

Do you send a résumé with this initial letter? There are varying opinions on this. Some people say yes because it helps the person learn about you and he or she may even want to pass it on to someone else.

Others say no because it gives the wrong impression. If you say you're not asking them for a job, sending a résumé may give the opposite message. Plus, at this point, you want to meet with this person, not have your résumé passed on to someone you don't know. I vote with the latter group.

What to Say in the Follow-up Phone Call to Someone You Don't Know

"Hello, Mr. Lincoln. This is Morris Adler. I was referred to you by Nancy Shmansy. I wrote you a letter that you probably received last week." (Pause, giving him time to recall your letter. If he needs more prompting, say something like:) "I'm the individual who will be moving to the San Diego area and Nancy referred me to you as someone who might be helpful to talk to.

"Nancy spoke very highly of you and told me about your background in financial services. As I shared in my letter, my background is in operations management in the financial services industry and I'm hoping to get more information about the industry in San Diego. I'll be visiting the week of April 20 and wondered if we could meet while I'm in town."

After you set a meeting be sure to give people your phone number and a local number of where you'll be staying when you visit. If they have to cancel, they can reach you. You need to make the most of your time when you're there. You'll be setting up these meetings as much as three to four weeks in advance, so I'd also urge you to confirm meetings as the date gets closer so that no one forgets you're coming.

If They Say No

If someone suggests you just talk on the phone, get them to reconsider. It's tough to get the type of feedback and result you want when the person isn't sitting across from you. You can't make an overall impression when your voice is the only thing the other person can observe. Remember, you want to get someone to get to know you, like you, and want to help you. Later, after you've met and are following up, other forms of communication like e-mail and memos are okay.

However, if you can't persuade someone to meet with you, then take what you can get—in this case, a phone conversation. But since you may not be prepared to talk and ask questions at that moment, since you were merely following up to your letter, ask if you can set another time—a specific phone meeting time.

When you do talk, set up the conversation the same way you would in person. Thank the person, reiterate the purpose for wanting to talk, refresh your listener's memory with your Move Mantra, and ask if they have any questions about your background. Then ask your questions.

Share what you've learned about the area and any businesses you're hoping to find out more about. Ask if they know about a firm you discovered in your list of brand-new businesses. Mention an article you read in their paper and ask if they know more about the head honcho who was quoted. He or she could be a friend or associate. Ask for the names of professional organizations in your field and whom to contact.

Depending on how the conversation is going, ask for suggestions of people you could talk to when you are in town. Since this person couldn't meet, they'll probably be willing to refer you to others. Be sure to get the phone number and address of any referrals—you're going to be writing them a letter next. And find out their relationship. Thank the person for their time and write a thank-you note—immediately.

◆ TALK TO REGULAR JOES

Employees Know the Ropes

Everybody (including me) tells you to talk to the decision makers—the people who run businesses and have the power to hire. You should. You should also talk to people who may not have the actual power to hire, but have the power to refer—and good reason for doing so.

More and more companies have employee referral programs— one way a company finds new staff. It's a creative recruiting strategy in which the company where you're employed offers you an incentive to recruit people you know to come work there. Some firms pay anywhere from $100 to $1,500 for each candidate who is eventually hired. The most I've heard of a company paying employees who recommend a new hire is $10,000 (that was Deloitte & Touche). It works because it's based on the tradition of how most people find jobs—word of mouth. It can also be a terrific morale booster for employees.

When I wrote about these human resource bounty programs in my column, one man wrote back saying he made $3,000 in the last eight months through his company's program. "My firm pays $1,000 for each person I refer and gets hired. And I feel good about helping these people," he wrote.

There are added benefits to you for talking with employees. When you hear about a job through an employee, you're in a better position to get inside information. A Stanford Graduate School of Business report also found that referral applicants are better timed than nonreferral applicants because you know when to submit your résumé. In interviews with bank recruiters, the coauthor of the report found that whenever the bank was short on applicants, the human resources staff would get on the phone and ask employees for referrals.

This also reinforces why you have to be able to present yourself well and demonstrate your professionalism. Even though there's a strong motivation for employees to refer good candidates, they don't want to feel responsible for referring someone who turns out to be a dud.

But, remember, unless you know of specific openings, when you're approaching these people too, don't put them in an awkward position by asking, "Do you know of any jobs?" You could get the opposite reaction that you want. If they don't know of any positions, they will probably feel badly they can't help you. But if you ask them questions about companies, the geographical area, growth in your industry—that type of thing—they can help. And if they know you, like you and want to help you, they'll do everything they can—including telling you about any job openings they do know about or hear about later.

Friends of the Family are Nice to Know

It's pretty darn nice to have a friendly face and home-cooked meal when you're in a strange place. When I was exploring working in San Francisco, I contacted a couple who my mother had gone to high school with forty-some years ago. They offered me directions, meals, a place to stay if I wanted, and referrals to other people in the community.

◆ CONTACT COMPANIES FOR ADVERTISED OR KNOWN POSITIONS

Your Objective

- To generate enough interest that they want to meet you
- To communicate your interest to live in their market
- To explain your overall qualifications and potential match

The best way to respond to an advertisement is to do whatever the ad tells you to do. If it says "Send a résumé and cover letter to Fred Fingerhut at P.O. Box 54321, Providence, RI 02904," do that.

If it's a position that's advertised on the net, it's likely you'll be instructed to e-mail a response or complete an application online. If someone tells you about a position that's open at the Freezing Floor Company, see if you can get the name of the decision maker for the department you'd work in. Then call him or her directly to find out how to proceed.

If someone tells you about a position and this person offers to contact the employer for you, be wary. First, you don't want this individual representing you. Second, you lose control. Be nice and appreciative. Thank the person. Then tell them you'd prefer to follow up on your own. But it sure wouldn't hurt for them to let their contact know you'll be calling. So suggest it.

Follow up to see if the employer is interested enough to bring you into town for an interview. If you can swing it, this could be one way to get to your target city. Odds are, though, you'll be on their schedule so you can't do much else while you're there.

If they haven't been willing to set up an interview, let them know you'll be in the area. (Smaller companies, especially, will hesitate or refuse to bear the cost of bringing you in for an interview.) If there's any interest in you at all, they'll usually be willing to meet if it's not costing them anything.

One more thing. I once got a letter from a reader of my column who was job hunting in the city where her husband had just been relocated. They hadn't moved yet, so she wanted to know: "Should I use a local address of the city we're moving to? I have heard that many companies won't even consider résumés with an out-of-town address."

I suppose there are some companies who, when noticing a return address from out of town, will just toss the envelope in the trash. And some employers may have doubts about your commitment level if you're not actually living there yet. So I guess it can't hurt. But I don't think it's necessary. If you're emphatic about why you're moving and when and if you're qualified for a position, an out-of-town address will not deter most employers.

◆ CONTACT SOMEONE YOU'VE READ ABOUT AND WANT TO MEET

Your Objective

- To introduce yourself
- To inform them of your overall objective to find a job there and your immediate objective to visit and meet with them
- To prepare them for your follow-up phone call to set a meeting
- To share your interest in knowing more about their company and industry or desire to work there

Here's where you can get creative. Based on the information that was in an article you read, use the data or this person's quotes to craft your letter.

Let's say you're in sales and the president of Leadbottom Plastics is quoted in the article as saying: "We're anxious to pump up our sales effort in Asia next quarter and plan to be on the cutting edge of our industry . . ." Use that as your "in."

Or you read a testimonial ad like the one I found in *Fortune*, in which the president of Stevedoring Services of America, the largest independent terminal operator and stevedore in the U.S. says, "Our market share of the West Coast, Atlantic Coast and Gulf Region is very high and that limits our ability to grow further in those areas. We realized that in order to continue to grow we had to explore business opportunities with our core competencies overseas."

He goes on to say how, as an organization, you must be able to react to new business ventures and potential projects quickly . . . and that they can "make decisions, form teams and pursue opportunities virtually overnight."

Great. Now you write a letter citing your experience in business development or finance—or whatever it is—with examples of how you've helped other companies make decisions, form teams, and pursue opportunities with lightning speed.

You may not get a response, let alone a meeting with the president himself. But it's very likely your letter will get passed on to someone in a decision-making role who will be willing to chat. Smart companies are always looking for good people.

Remember the woman I told you about in Chapter 2 who was investigating a move into a *new* industry *and* location? She dug up issues of the local business newspaper. She wrote the president of a company in the industry she was targeting who was quoted in an article, citing some of his comments. Her letter was forwarded to his senior vice president who saw her when she visited their city. He offered her a job.

Your goal, when you do meet with someone you've read or heard about, depends on what you said in your letter. If you know a lot about their company and are direct about your interest in working there, your goal is to talk about how your skills and background can meet their needs and communicate your commitment to moving.

If you're like my client who had a dream to work for Dell Computer, your goal is to make that very clear to them and demonstrate what you can do for the company.

If you wrote you just wanted to meet to learn more about their company and explore how you might fit into their industry, your goal is to get information and share why you want it.

ALMOST READY TO SET SAIL

See what I mean when I say this is a process? This particular part of the process—calling and meeting with local folks, calling and writing people in your target area, and setting up meetings—can take between one and three weeks. Depends on how hard you work at it. The harder you work, the quicker it will happen.

Now you have people who didn't know you before and who like you and want to help you. You have a set of cheerleaders back home and in the place where you're headed. And you have a whole new group of people who you're going to meet when you get to your target destination. They should all understand your career objective, rationale, and commitment to moving—since you did such a good job of positioning yourself.

By the way, did I mention you're doing all of this from home? And what did it cost you? Basically, long-distance phone calls, postage, letterhead and envelopes. That's small potatoes.

Now let's get you ready to make this first trip.

Thank-you letter to someone in your hometown (if you know the person well, it can be handwritten)

Glenn Garduci
6889 Mystic Way North
Jacksonville, FL 32203

June 11, 1999

Dear Marcia:

Thank you for your great advice on conducting my job search in Boston. You not only gave me useful information on businesses I want to approach, but invaluable tips on how to get around and where to stay.

I especially appreciate your insight into Medipax, a company that's the big player in my field. I will contact Marie Shribner and Brad Pittsky this week.

As promised, I'll keep you updated on my progress and call when I get back in town in August.

Again, thank you for your help.

Sincerely,

Glenn Garduci

Letter to someone you've been referred to and don't know:

**Morris Adler
5544 Mifflin Way
Indianapolis, IN 46205
(317) 222-9222**

March 28, 1999

Mr. Ismael Lincoln
President
Fargo First National Bank
120 East Cerita Avenue
San Diego, CA 92883

Dear Mr. Lincoln:

Your former neighbor, Nancy Shmancy, suggested I contact you. Nancy, who lives next door to my wife and me here in Indiana, has been very helpful by providing me with insight into the San Diego area, where we plan to move in the next six months.

Since you and I are in the same industry, I am hoping you would be willing to meet when I visit San Diego next month. I'd like to get your input on the financial institutions in the area, as well as your advice on how my background fits into the San Diego market.

I have worked for First and Foremost Inc., the second largest credit card issuer in the state, for nine years as the vice president of operations. We were recently bought by a competitor who is closing our operation here. My wife and I planned to move to the San Diego area some time in the future. With the closing of the company and our children grown, the time is right now.

My objective is to find a position where I can use my extensive experience in operations management and customer service. I have an eighteen-year track record in leading complex organizations in the financial services industry through change and overseeing day-to-day operations and strategic planning.

I plan to visit from April 20 to May 2 and will call you next week to set up a convenient time to meet. Nancy sends her warm regards.

Sincerely,

Morris Adler

Letter to someone you've been referred to and don't know:

Louisa May Dalcott
587 Alhambra Place
Alexandria, VA 22330

Ms. Freida Kischka
Media Consultants
2310 Lincoln Park West
Chicago, IL 60613

May 10, 1999

Dear Ms. Kischka:

I was referred to you by my college professor Louis Kandinsky, who said you are very knowledgeable about the broadcasting industry in the Chicago area.

As a recent graduate from Northwestern University with a degree in telecommunications, in the fall I plan to move back to Chicago, where I hope to work in broadcasting. My two internships in the news departments at WJBK-TV in Southfield, Michigan, and WMAR-TV in Baltimore, Maryland, helped me confirm my strong interest to work in the research area.

Your thoughts, feedback, and advice on how I can achieve my career objective would be greatly appreciated. Mr. Kandinsky said that you are a very busy person, so I promise not to take more than twenty minutes of your time. I also want to clarify that I would not expect you to know of a position for me, but I know that I would benefit greatly by talking to you.

Would it be possible for us to meet when I am in Chicago between June 2 and 15? I will call your office next week.

Thank you.

Sincerely,

Louisa May Dalcott

Response to advertised or known position:

Sydney Slicker
333 S. Denver
Tulsa, OK 74118
(918) 592-0000

March 3, 1999

Mr. Leroy Toomcake
Arlington Quids & Prodometers
90088 Randall Park
Davenport, IA 52807

Dear Mr. Toomcake:

If you're looking for someone with a broad understanding of manufacturing technology, who thinks globally, understands how to manage the nuts and bolts of a business, and has a successful profit-making track record, I am such a person.

I am currently exploring how to contribute these qualities and a wealth of knowledge and experience in manufacturing, distribution and international trade to a firm like yours in the Davenport area. When I read your advertisement for the position of Director of Operations, it struck me as a good match between your needs and my qualifications.

Your firm's focus on change integration is of particular interest to me since I have successfully lead several initiatives at my present firm to adapt to massive market changes while increasing sales and improving profitability.

Perhaps it would make sense for us to discuss a potential match. I will contact you next week.

Thank you.

Sincerely,

Sydney Slicker

Keeping it open like this may result in the company paying for your trip. If that doesn't happen, let them know when you'll be in town so you can schedule an interview.

Letter to someone you've read about, researched their company and want to talk to about a position when you're in town:

Brad Osherwitz
46 East Norwalk Street
Madison, WI 53713

February 8, 1999

Ms. Michelle Akea
President
Akeaware Inc.
One Plaza Way
Austin, Texas

Dear Ms. Akea:

When I read about your vision to have a global presence by the twenty-first century, it seemed as if there might be a match between your needs and my expertise.

I am currently exploring how to contribute my experience in innovative marketing and international trade to a progressive company in the Austin area.

My qualifications include ten years working with two start-up firms where I created and implemented long-range marketing plans, catapulting both companies into market leadership positions. I also have a successful track record in international trade, helping both companies meet their global goals.

I am committed to moving to Austin by the end of this year, since my wife's company is relocating its headquarters in November. I will be in the area from March 15 to 30. Since your goals include an international focus with an emphasis on innovative marketing, wouldn't it make sense for us to discuss a potential match between your needs and my qualifications? I will call early next week to explore your interest in meeting during my visit to Austin.

Thank you.

Sincerely,

Brad Osherwitz

Letter to recruiter:

Merton McDuff
9897 Lola Bridges
Baton Rouge, LA 70822
(504) 767-0000

April 15, 1999

Mr. Marvin Shmarvin
Excellente Recruiters, Inc.
14 Bridgewater Avenue
Syracuse, NY 13299

Dear Mr. Shmarvin:

If one of your clients is looking for a creative leader with a strong marketing and sales background in consumer products and services, please consider me as a qualified candidate.

I have twelve years of experience in building sales-driven organizations while reducing costs, improving quality, and enhancing short-term operations. My expertise includes developing innovative marketing strategies and business plans that increased my present employer's sales by 100 percent in three months.

My qualifications include consumer and trade promotion, new product roll-outs, development of distribution channels, and market research. A few of my recent accomplishments are that I:

• Developed a distribution strategy and led roll-out of new product that took sales from $200,000 to $6 million.

• Created an international marketing strategy that generated $4.5 million in sales in three months.

My résumé gives more details of my extensive experience as a marketing executive.

My wife has accepted a position at Spelman College in Atlanta, so we will be moving to the Atlanta area in early June. I am seeking a position in sales and marketing with responsibility for new product development and international marketing and sales.

I will call you to follow up and discuss whether my credentials meet any of your clients' needs.

Thank you.

Sincerely,

Merton McDuff

4

PLOTTING YOUR FIRST VISIT

You've got anywhere from two to three weeks now before you head east, north, south, or west, wherever it is you're heading to for your first all-important visit. This reminds me that it's time to establish exactly what you're trying to accomplish in this initial visit.

This may surprise you, but it's not to get a job. No, siree. Now I'm not saying you won't *get* a job offer (although it's highly unlikely), but your main reason for going on this trip is *not* to come back with a live offer. It's to:

1. Get information about the community, industries, and companies
2. Meet new people and get them to know you, like you, and want to help you
3. Hold meetings with people to gather information and feedback and, if possible, have job interviews
4. Weave your way into the community and penetrate the job market
5. Get a better idea of how you like the area as a place to live and work

MORE NAGGING

For heaven's sake, you're not ready to accept a new job yet! You've just begun your search. And you don't want to take the first offer that comes along now do you? The odds of getting an offer—a super-duper one at least—are nil anyway. Plus the interview process for one job can take awhile—anywhere from two to five or more interviews. (In case you do get an offer on Day 1, I talk about how to handle that without risking a good opportunity in Chapter 5.)

You may learn of openings while you're there, but unless you've shopped around, you have nothing to compare them to. I know it's very flattering when someone offers you a job. But you can't wimp out here. Your goal is not just to get *any* job. It's to get a position that:

- Uses your skills
- Challenges you
- Pays you what you're worth
- Is in an environment and culture that's comfortable to you
- Is in a company with a management you like and whose values are aligned with yours

Remember we talked about that way back in Chapter 1? If you're going to be smart about this, you have to think in steps. Even though you're finally getting out of the house, this visit is another step, not the end result.

So, back to what you need to do while you're still home.

1. CLEAN UP YOUR ROOM: IN THIS CASE, YOUR JOB SEARCH ACTIVITY

If you've been doing everything I've told you, you have a ton of data. What are you doing with it? Do you have zillions of pieces of paper plastered with Post-it notes bulging out of a folder? Are they scattered on a desk? Is some of it on the floor of your car, in the bathroom, or next to your night stand? No good.

For one thing, unless this information is well organized, you're going to be overwhelmed with all the data and things you're supposed to do and you'll throw up your hands in frustration and shout, "I can't do this! I'm doomed to live in Hackensack for the rest of my life."

Two, you have to lug this information with you on your trip.

Three, you have to stay focused on what you're trying to accomplish each step of the way.

Here's my suggestion:

Get an old-fashioned three-ring binder and put the whole shebang in it. Even if all this information is on your computer or a laptop that you're taking with you, you'll need hard copy of correspondence and lists you've compiled; plus, you'll want to be able to reference ads and articles you've researched. A big old fat binder is a logical way to organize it all and keep it on the seat of the car as you drive around and check out the place. Get some of those tabs that create sections in your binder and let you easily identify what you want—whether it's hard data, directions, or inspiration. I've listed below my recommendations for the type of information you put in it. Let's call this binder and its contents your *Move Manifesto*.

YOUR *MOVE MANIFESTO* SECTIONS:

◆ MY RATIONALE AND COMMITMENT FOR MOVING

This is the information you wrote in Chapter 1. Writing it down and carrying it with you will help you stay focused. You'll be glad you have it when those itty-bitty doubts creep into your mind. Or someone says, "You want to move? Whaddaya crazy?"

This information includes:

- *Your* reason for moving statement
- The list of people your move affects
- Your Checklist of What's Important to *You*

◆ My Goal and Strategy

This is what you wrote in Chapter 2. This too will help you stay on target in case you stray off course. This includes:

- Your specific career goal
- The steps you'll take to get there

I'd also create sections to organize all the data you've collected. Use whatever format works best for you. Of course, I've got some ideas as to how to do that. Feel free to steal them.

◆ Research

This is all that stuff you dug up in Chapter 2.

- Articles and newsletters
- Data about companies and the people in them
- Cost of living, crime rate, climate—that type of information
- Lists of companies you've compiled or bought

◆ People

These are those lists you made in Chapter 2.

- People in the place where you live now (write down who you met and when)
- People you already know in your targeted area
- People you want to meet

Make sure you have everyone's address and phone number. You may need to contact someone back home or in your target city.

◆ MOVE MANTRA

This is that brief, concise explanation of who you are, why you want to move, and how committed you are—which we explored in Chapter 3.

◆ TARGET COMPANIES

This is that list you created in Chapter 3 to have ready to show to people in meetings. Remember that? You compiled it through your research and talking with people who know the area.

◆ ADVERTISEMENTS

If you've answered any ads, copy and paste each one on a piece of paper along with your cover letter, responses you've received, and any other pertinent information. Include ads you responded to on the net.

◆ LIST OF JOB BANKS AND DATABASES WHERE YOU'VE POSTED YOUR RÉSUMÉ

These are those places on the net where you put your résumé.

◆ QUESTIONS YOU NEED ANSWERED

You're not going to find out everything you want to know in your initial stage of research. In fact, the more you learn, the more questions you'll have. Keep a running list of things you want to know. This will be a handy reference when you think about how people can help you and when you are formulating specific questions you want to ask in your upcoming meetings.

◆ REFERRALS

Whenever someone gives you a name of someone else to talk to, add them to your Referral List. Remember what I said in Chapter 3 about keeping people updated? (Write down their names, addresses, and phone numbers so it's easy to stay in contact and you will have no excuse for not doing it.) You can include more information, like who referred you and their connection to that person, what you know about them, what you learned from them (once you meet), and the date and nature of your follow up. Or you can put that kind of data on a form I'll talk about in a minute.

◆ CORRESPONDENCE

Include copies of correspondence you've had with everyone since you started this process: thank-you letters, requests for meetings, letters to recruiters, companies, and chambers of commerce.

◆ DIRECTIONS

If you're driving yourself around, you'll need precise directions on how to get to and from your various appointments, to neighborhoods you want to check out, to where you're staying—that sort of thing.

◆ LIST OF APPOINTMENTS FOR THIS TRIP

Create a list with the person's name address, phone, fax, and e-mail and date and time of your meeting.

Optional:

- Key points to cover on the phone

This will help you be short and sweet and stick to the point when you're calling people to make appointments.

This is Very Important

Put plenty copies of your résumé in the pockets of your binder. Keep them clean and flat so the corners don't get dog-earred. Make copies of anything that came to you via fax—the print fades on fax paper.

There's one more thing I want you to create and keep in your Move Manifesto. It's a form that lets you track your meetings and what takes place in them. These meetings, after all, are the crux of your job search. You've gone to a gosh-awful lot of trouble to get these meetings, will garner lots of valuable information from them, and are building the seeds of important relationships. You need to have a way to record this information, which you'll use on this trip and in the future.

Believe me, you're not going to remember half of it if you don't do this. I don't care how good your memory is. If you're having several meetings a day, driving around in a strange town, learning new directions and meeting new people, you're going to forget who told you what if you don't capture it on paper—and as soon after the meeting as possible. See pages 97–99 for a sample form I created that lets you record it all.

While I'm talking about forms, here's an idea for one more that will really help you be thorough, stay organized, and quickly evaluate what you learn about companies as you go through this process. It's an expanded version of your Target Company List. Let's call it your Target Company Profile form. It's a way to track information about your target companies as you get it through research and by talking to people. It acts as a supplement to your Target Company List.

For example, let's say the Crunchy French Fry Company is on your target list. You'd create a separate sheet of paper for them with details such as a brief description of the type of business, names of key managers and employees, what you know or learned about each person, a description of why this company could be a fit for you, specific facts you've learned or impressions you've gotten about the company (and who told you), projects in process there, long- and short-term company goals, and specific technologies the company uses.

Some of this data will be on your Meeting Record Form. So at the end of each day, you can transfer the information to this Target Company Profile. As you get more data, you add it to the profile. Later on, when you're evaluating whether you want to pursue a potential job opportunity or a firm offer, you'll have the information you need right there in front of you to make an informed decision. (See sample form on pages 98–99.)

Complete one of these forms after every meeting.

MEETING RECORD FORM

Today's date _____

Person I met with _____ Title _____

Company _____ Address _____

Phone _____ Fax _____ E-mail _____

Who referred me _____

May I use his or her name? _____

Their relationship _____

What I know about this person _____

_____

_____

Objective of meeting _____

_____

Questions I want to ask _____

_____

_____

_____

_____

_____

_____

_____

What I learned today:

Industry/ies we discussed:

Referrals I got:

Action I take next:

Complete one of these forms for each of your target companies as you learn more about the firm:

TARGET COMPANY PROFILE

Company: _____

Address: _____

Phone: _____ Fax: _____ E-mail: _____

Type of business: _____

_____

Who referred me: Their relationship:

_____   _____

Key managers:

Name _____ Title _____ Description _____

_____   _____   _____

Name _____ Title _____ Description _____

_____   _____   _____

Employee contacts:

Name _____ Title _____ Description _____

_____   _____   _____

Name _____ Title _____ Description _____

_____   _____   _____

Why company could be a fit: _____

_____

_____

Specific facts learned: _____

_____

_____

TARGET COMPANY PROFILE continued

Impressions heard about company and from whom: _____
_____
_____

Projects in process at company: _____
_____
_____

Long- and short-term company goals: _____
_____
_____

Specific technologies used there: _____
_____
_____

2. GET A RIDE AND A NICE PLACE TO STAY

How are you getting there? By plane, train, or car? If you're flying, purchase your tickets and double-check that the dates are correct when you receive confirmation. I have been known to go up to the ticket counter on a return flight from out of town to discover that my ticket was for a flight that left the day before. I had no one but myself to blame.

If you're trying to save money, now is the time to cash in frequent flyer miles.

◆ GETTING AROUND

Reserve a rental car if you'll need one. Get maps for getting to the city and getting around once you're there. Check with the AAA if you're a member. There are several free, online services that let you create maps of how to get to your destination. Expedia.com will give you complete directions from your starting point to your destination. For example, when I typed in Detroit as my starting point and Pittsburgh as my destination, it told me I'd be driving 274.3 miles and it would take 4 hours 29 minutes. It showed which highways to take, which direction I'd be heading at all times, at what point of the trip I'd enter Ohio, then Pennsylvania, and the exact exits to take. Pretty nifty, huh?

This site also lets you locate businesses, get weather forecasts, and access the lowest published airfare rate.

Another online service that creates maps is www.movequest. com. You can map out exactly how to get from your hotel to a meeting by typing in where you are and the address of your destination. On this site you can also estimate the mileage of your move and calculate moving expenses based on interstate moving costs. See the Appendix for more of these services, which offer everything from maps to news about construction delays.

Check out the various modes of transportation the area offers. For instance, if you were headed to San Francisco, on the net you could find everything from a downtown parking guide and tips on avoiding traffic congestion to parking meter rates for Fisherman's Wharf as compared to downtown, where to get free shuttles, and easy ways to pay your traffic citations (www.ci.sf.ca.us/info.htm).

◆ WHERE TO STAY

As far as accommodations go, you've got several options. The cheapest is to stay with people you know. The downside is that you can be distracted from your mission if you're staying with friends or family. If you do stay with people you know, make it very clear that this is not a vacation or sightseeing trip. They may or may not understand. Use your judgment. It might be easier just to make dinner plans with them while you're there so you can stay focused on business.

Hotels run the gamut, of course—from swanky to sleazy. In addition to the regular hotel or motel, consider an extended-stay hotel. They cater to people who stay five or more nights and the accommodations usually have kitchens, suites with a separate bedroom or at least a sitting area, a work area and dataport phone, and access to laundry areas. Some have separate living areas and bedrooms. According to *USA Today*, rates range from $25 a day in low-cost areas such as parts of Texas to $92 a day in metropolitan areas like Chicago. The longer you stay, the lower the daily rate. Weekly rates range from $200 to $600. Extended-stay hotels include Extended Stay America, AmeriSuites, Homestead Village, MainStay, Staybridge Suites, and Residence Inns.

Many hotels now offer the things you need when you're doing business: portable phones, in-room personal computers and high-speed Internet access. Some hotels such as Marriott, the Hilton's mid-priced Hilton Garden Inn Hotels, and ITT Sheraton are creating in-room offices equipped with multiline phones, ergonomic chairs, special lighting, and e-mail. Some Hiltons have Internet kiosks in their lobbies. Some also allow guests to check e-mail using wireless infrared keyboards. The Appendix gives more resources.

◆ Stretching Your Dollar

Cheapskate newsletter is a good source of information for bargains. Their address is www.cyberthug.com. Through one of their links I found www.econet.org/frugal/ which gives a guide to city and metro areas' low-cost goods and services. You'll find out who has the cheapest gasoline prices in the Boston area and lists of inexpensive places to eat in Boulder, Colorado, Chicago, and Washington, D.C.

3. NO WINGING IT: PREP FOR YOUR MEETINGS

Since your goal is to get people's input on the business climate, get information that will help you focus your search, get referrals, find out about specific companies, establish yourself as tops in your field and someone an employer would love to have at their company, and potentially discover jobs before they hit the newspaper ads, you need to:

◆ THINK THROUGH QUESTIONS YOU WANT TO ASK EACH PERSON

These will vary, depending on what this person does and how your referral thought they could help you.

For example, let's say your friend Natasha refers you to Mitchell Martinez in Portland, Oregon, where you're headed, because you and Mitchell are in the same field—human resources. Although Mitchell is a consultant and works for himself, he works closely with many companies. Natasha feels Mitchell would be able to tell you about firms in the area who have human resource departments and other consultants.

Natasha, however, is a dental hygienist and doesn't know much about what Mitchell does. (They met in a tanning salon when they both lived in Montana and became good friends.) So, assuming you weren't able to discover ahead of time more specifically what Mitchell does, find out the information at the beginning of the meeting so you know what questions to ask him. Some logical questions to start off with would be: Exactly what kind of consulting do you do? Do you specialize in compensation and benefits? Training? Leadership development?

The conversation will flow from there. Questions might include: What types of companies do you do this work for? What kinds of human resource departments do they have? Have you noticed any particular areas that companies are lacking in or where problems aren't being addressed? Are you familiar with the Society for Human Resources chapter here in Portland? Who would I contact to get more information? Do you know of any job focus groups here? (If the person doesn't know what they are, explain. Most likely, if the contact doesn't know what they are, he or she won't know of any. But you never know. Your description could ring a bell.)

Show him that list of companies you compiled and say: "Here is a list of some companies I'd like to talk to while I'm here. What do you think? Can you tell me anything about them or suggest the best way to approach them? Can you think of any obstacles I'd run into? Could you recommend any other people for me to talk to as we did here today?"

◆ BE READY TO TALK ABOUT YOURSELF IN MORE DETAIL

You created your Move Mantra in Chapter 3 and it will help out greatly in these meetings, but be prepared to go into more detail. For one thing, most of these people don't know you, so they'll probably want more details. Second, you never know when someone you're sitting across from may be considering you for a job in his company. (I get into that later in this chapter.)

Let's look at how you can expand your Move Mantra. The parts of your Move Mantra are:

Who You Are

Besides an overview of your career and your objective, you can expand it by talking about your strengths, what you're knowledgeable about, where you have worked in the past, and the kinds of responsibilities you've had.

If you're making a career change, be ready to briefly explain how your skills transfer and why you're interested in this new field.

Be able to cite specific accomplishments (ways you've been valuable) in your field.

You can share some of your personal characteristics that make you effective. These would be attributes like being detail-oriented, flexible, good in a crisis, politically astute, fair, resourceful—that sort of thing.

All this information gives someone a better idea of who you are.

Why You Want to Move and How Committed You Are

To expand this be prepared to give more incidentals about how you chose this particular area to move to, who you know there, if you've ever spent time there, what you like about the area, and how you're conducting your job search and planning to move.

Put all of this into what I call your three-minute commercial. This is a brief, rehearsed (not memorized) presentation that tells who you are, what kind of position you're looking for, why you're looking—and specifically in this geographical area, and why someone would want to hire you.

Sample Three-Minute Commercial

"My background is in computers and business applications. I've worked for Innovative Information in Durham, North Carolina, for seven years, where I have been a systems analyst. I work closely with our clients in ascertaining their needs, then interpreting those needs for our design team. Much of my experience prior to that was at a firm that developed software for financial analysts. There, I gave presentations to our clients that explained the software's technical features and I acted as the liaison between the software developers and the product management teams.

"I enjoy what I do and would like to stay in this field, but I would like to continue my career in the Northwest. I took a vacation here in Seattle last year and fell in love with the area. Since I have cousins here, I've been back twice and decided that I want to relocate.

"So my objective is to find a position where I can contribute my knowledge of computers and business applications and skills to communicate and write about technical information in a simple manner.

"An example of how I've used my strengths successfully is

when I was working with a new client in Puerto Rico. They needed software for a new accounting process. I talked with them, analyzed their needs, and wrote documentation that explained their situation to our software developers. The result was that our client has software that has increased their accuracy by 90 percent and cut their processing time in half. They have since given us $5 million new business.

"I'd be most comfortable in a smaller company where I can get involved in other aspects of the firm and have the opportunity to build the business."

When will you use this—in part or in its entirety? I'll get into that next.

◆ BE READY TO SET THE AGENDA AND RUN THE MEETING

You are the one who asked for the meeting, so don't expect the other person to lead the way. That's not to say that someone won't try to take control. In that case, you need to go with it—to a point. Make sure your objective for holding the meeting is met. I've had clients who came out of these meetings saying they got nothing out of it. When I asked why, they say things like, "She just wanted to talk about her business," or "he just asked me questions about what it's like to live in Chicago." Whose fault was that?

It's your responsibility to steer the direction of the conversation. Hop to it. Sometimes, out of nervousness or if you're not taking the reins, the other person will. If the discussion isn't going the way you want, change the course. Put yourself in the other person's shoes. Most likely this is someone who wants to help as much as he or she can. But at this very moment, this person may not know exactly how. Help him. Steer the conversation so that it's productive.

Here is how your meeting might unfold. Of course it may not go exactly like this, but these are the elements I'd like you to incorporate to get the most out of your meeting.

1. Shoot the Breeze

Like the first seconds and moments of any conversation, you need to warm up to each other, so keep it light. Comment on the office, the weather, how beautiful the city is, how good the directions were—anything that's not controversial. Mention your referral that got you to this person—if it's okay with this original contact. Thank them for their time again.

2. Say It Like It Is: State Your Objective for This Meeting

You're reestablishing the purpose of this meeting to help it stay on track and set the tone. Say something like:

"As I shared in my letter and on the phone, I wanted to meet you to get more information on the financial services industry here in San Diego. Nan had so many good things to say about you and felt you could be of help. Since I wrote to you, I've done even more research, so I also have some specific companies I'd like to ask you about. I want to also reiterate that I don't expect you to know of any jobs for me. I'm here to get your advice."

3. Spell Out Your Background and Objective

This is the perfect spot for your three-minute commercial. It depends on who this person is and how familiar he or she is with your industry as to the kind of detail you give. Get into it by saying: "First, I'd thought I could give you a little more background on myself . . ." Most people will be happy to hear this, since they're wondering about you. Remember, they want to know who you are, why you want to move, and how committed you are to making this move.

Now you may not get through every point of your three-minute commercial. The person may interrupt you and ask a question. That's swell. It means he or she is listening. You're having a conversation. Just be sure to get in the important particulars at some point.

4. Get Curious: Ask Prepared Questions

Now you're ready to get input. Start asking the questions you wrote down in advance. Take notes. Ask for clarification if you need it. Converse. Show the list of companies you compiled. Ask if he knows about them and if the companies fit the profile of the type of firm you're interested in.

5. Don't Be Shy: Ask for Referrals

If this person told you about a new development in your industry, ask if he knows of someone you could talk to to get more detail. If he talked about a particular company, ask if he knows someone there you could talk to to get advice. If he mentioned a professional association, ask whom to contact for more information. The person may have offered referrals during the course of your conversation. That's terrific. If not, ask for them now.

Be sure to ask if it's okay to use his name as the person who referred you. Assuming he says yes, ask how he knows the person, what he knows about them, and why he thinks they'd be good to talk to. One of my clients got so many referrals he had to start being picky about who he would meet with. He was able to pick and choose by knowing more about the referral. Nice problem to have, huh?

If you didn't get any referrals, don't come unglued. Maybe the person just can't think of anyone. Ask if it's okay to call back later to see if he may have thought of someone.

If you haven't given him a résumé yet, be sure to leave one with him now.

6. Wind Down and Wrap It Up

Thank the person again for his time, advice, referrals—anything he shared. Tell him you'll keep him updated. Get his business card.

7. Write Your Thank-you Note

That very day after your meeting, write your thank-you note and mail it. It's preferable if it's typed. But if that's not possible, handwrite it and mail it on the note cards that you had printed up. (I'll talk about this more later in this chapter.)

Don't get into the habit of writing meaningless thank-you notes that say zilch and sound like you got them out of a book. Ones that go like this:

> Dear Ms. Frimpy:
>
> Thank you very much for your time today. I really appreciated your advice and referrals and will keep you updated on my progress.
>
> Sincerely,
>
>
> Marcus McLarkus

Tailor your note to each person and be sincere. Make reference to the advice that was most helpful. Mention the referrals you'll be contacting. You'll find sample thank-you letters in Chapter 6 (as examples of tone and content, not to copy word for word).

Practice holding mock meetings before you go on the road. I'm sure you remember that I wanted you to have some real meetings in your hometown—to practice as well as get information. But if you haven't done that, practice at home with a friend or family member now. Outline the steps I just showed you and follow them. Do it even if you hate role playing. You'll thank me later.

Tips

• If you told them you'd keep the meeting to a half hour, notice when you're near the half hour point and say something like: "I promised to only take a half hour of your time, so I'll close with this question . . ." If they say they've got more time, that's another story.

• A lot of people tell me they think it's best to start off by asking the person they're meeting with all about herself. They think it's very slick to get all chummy and ask things like: "How long have you been doing this? What got you started?" They rationalize that it's a good way to get the person talking and shows you're interested in her—even if you aren't.

I think it's a good way to steer the meeting in the wrong direction. You're not there to learn about her career. If it's relevant, or will help you know what to ask, fine. Otherwise ask only about data that's relevant. She's busy. This is not a gabfest. Besides, it's insincere. You stated the purpose of this meeting in your letter; stick to it.

• When I say keep the person updated, I don't just mean in a couple of weeks. If something significant happens later in the week that would be of interest to this person, call her while you're still in town and tell her. For instance, if she referred you to a company and you discovered you're just what the company needs, share the news. You might even want to talk further with her.

This is how you build meaningful relationships.

◆ WISE UP FOR JOB INTERVIEWS

Even if you haven't set up a single interview for an actual job, be ready for one. You never know when one of these other kinds of meetings can turn into a job interview. Here are some ways that can happen:

• You're doing such a great job of getting people to know you and like you, and such a bang up job of showing how you're tops in your field, they might decide to create a position for you at their company.

• Your questions or description of what you can do have helped them see where they may need someone like you.

• They may have known of a job opening at their company all along; now that they like you, they're considering you as a candidate.

• They may know of an opening at someone else's company and tell you about it. Or they could call up a colleague after you leave and say, "Hey, I just met someone who's moving here from Georgia. She's got a sales and marketing background. Isn't that what you need?" Then you get a call from this person later.

In Chapter 5, I'll talk about clues you'll get to know it's gone from an information-seeking meeting to a job interview. While we're on this subject, I want to emphasize again that you should definitely try to set up any job interviews for positions you know about. Be aggressive about calling back companies whose ads you've answered or if you learned of an opening another way. Remind them that you'll be in town on such-and-such dates. Reiterate your commitment to moving to their area. If you set up an interview, ask for a copy of the job description. This will help you prepare for the interview.

WHAT TO PACK

◆ OFFICE STUFF

Take items that will let you set up a mini office away from home, including a computer or laptop (or you can rent one once you get to your destination; look up computer rental in the Yellow Pages). You'll need this to write thank-you notes and other correspondence while you're out of town. You may also want to check your e-mail.

You'll need envelopes, stamps, paper clips, copies of your résumé, and computer disks. You can use a printer (and a computer for that matter) at a copy place like Kinko's.

Order some note cards with your name printed on them and matching envelopes with your home address. You can use these to handwrite your thank-you notes if you don't have a computer. They can be also be used to express a quick thank-you to someone for something else besides the meeting, or for updating a person on your progress.

Some people print up business cards with their name, address, and a phrase that describes them or their field of expertise. I don't feel strongly one way or the other about it. If you want to hand out a business card, that's fine.

◆ APPROPRIATE CLOTHES

You're going to a business meeting, so dress the part: a suit, a jacket and tie or skirt and jacket. Even if people dress casually at a company where you have a meeting, dress like a professional. Check the weather as your visit gets closer. This will help you know exactly what weight clothing to take. Check the list of weather sources I give in the Appendix.

IF THEY'RE PAYING

If your spouse or significant other has a job offer in the place you're investigating, this may be a slightly different kind of first visit. Your mate may not have decided whether to take the job, so the potential employer is paying for a "let's look and see how we like the place before we make a decision" visit. Your ability to get a job there may influence you and your mate's decision. So I still urge you to hold these meetings while you're there so you can gather information.

On the other hand, your partner could have decided to move for a job. The company may be paying for you to see the community and to start house hunting. In either situation, his or her company is paying for the trip. Make the most of it.

If your mate's company has a spouse relocation program (some offer this benefit even if you're not married) use it. These are programs that help you, the trailing spouse or partner, find employment. Most will help you set up the kinds of meetings we've been talking about as well as work with you on getting to know the market and how you fit in. It's likely your mate's company will pay for several visits to an area.

ANYTHING ELSE ON THE AGENDA?

Depending on what you want to know and how much time you've got, consider scheduling other types of meetings on this trip. One woman I know set up a meeting with a realtor during her first visit. Another person had an appointment with a rabbi so he could learn more about the Jewish community in the area. That was a key factor on his livability profile (we discussed this in Chapter 1). While another one of my clients was holding meetings to get information about companies, his spouse visited schools in the area.

Whether you're going on this trip by yourself or with a spouse or friend, envision how you see the trip unfolding. If you want to do more than have meetings to talk about your job search, what is it? At what point in the trip will you do that and how much time will you devote?

Make a list of everything you want to accomplish, what you want to see, and who you want to talk to.

BEFORE YOU HIT THE ROAD

Make sure you're organized with your Move Manifesto, you've got your Move Mantra and three-minute commercial down, you've brushed up on your interview skills, got a ride there and back, know where you're staying, who and what you're seeing, and what you want to accomplish. Get someone to feed the fish. Confirm meeting dates and times.

The time is ripe. Let's hit the road.

OTHER THINGS TO ACCOMPLISH WORKSHEET

Jot down names and numbers, and record your impressions of the following:

Realtors (If you were taken to see any houses or apartments, what were your impressions of those?): _____

_____

_____

_____

Area churches or synagogues; religious leaders: _____

_____

_____

_____

Chamber of Commerce: _____

_____

_____

_____

Local schools and educators: _____

_____

_____

_____

Cultural activities: _____

_____

_____

_____

Sports events: _____

_____

_____

_____

5

ROUND ONE

Once you've arrived at your destination, you need to take care of the important stuff first. Which as everyone knows is to find:

- A joint with great coffee where you can relax and read the newspaper, review your notes, and regroup during slack times
- A good Chinese or Thai takeout that doesn't use MSG
- A friendly gas station

If you're driving, you'll not only need gasoline, but occasional directions. Find a place where the attendants know how to get around side streets and freeways. In these days of self-serve gas stations with clerks who scarcely leave their minimarts, this can be more difficult than you think.

- A couple of places that offer good public phone facilities

These could be a relatively quiet hotel lobby or a spot in a building with phones that have a ledge or an area where you can take notes. If you don't have a cellular or digital phone, there will be times when you'll be out and about and need to call people to confirm times, follow up or make appointments.

- A library

This is not only a good source of information when you need it, it's a good quiet place to write letters and complete your Interview Record Forms.

- A photocopy shop such as Kinko's or a full-service office business store

There will probably be a time when you need to make copies, use a printer, or buy supplies. Stake out one that is open twenty-four hours a day if possible.

• A post office branch or Mail Boxes Etc. store

You never know when you may need to wrap and mail a package.

• A way to get and retrieve messages

Either get voice mail at your hotel, bring an answering machine, or set up e-mail while you're there. If you're staying with friends, you need to create an arrangement for you to get your messages.

• Next-day dry cleaners

This is handy in case you spill your Chinese takeout on your clothes.

• A place for quiet reflection

After a hectic day of driving to meetings, finding your way around, talking to strangers, and being on your best behavior, you could use a place to unwind. Find a park or quiet place where you can sit and reflect.

MORE ON LOGISTICS

It also can't hurt to drive around and get a feel for the area in relationship to where your appointments will be. This will help you gauge how much time you'll need to get places.

Try to create a schedule where you get up at the same time every day and have a routine. Bodies as well as minds like order. A routine will help you feel more at home.

The number of meetings you'll have in a day will depend on the size and layout of your market. When I was checking out job opportunities in San Francisco, it was enough to schedule two meetings a day. Sometimes that was even pushing it. The area is so spread out, I had to figure in hours of driving and sometimes a combination of driving and public transportation from one place to the next. Eventually, I figured out not to schedule different meetings on opposite sides of the Bay and the times of day it was unwise to get on the Bay Bridge.

It pays to check out a web site of the area before you get to your location, as I discussed in Chapter 4. But once you're there, you'll figure out the best routes and short cuts. Once you're settled, go over your Move Mantra, review your schedule, the six steps that you'd like to see take place in your meeting, and confirm any meetings for the week if you didn't get ahold of someone before you left. Now you're ready for your first round of meetings.

WHAT CAN HAPPEN IN A DAY

In Chapter 4 we talked in detail about what you want to get out of these face-to-face meetings you've scheduled and the six steps that will take place—more or less—so I won't repeat it here. But I do want to remind you what to use to your advantage and what to bring with you to meetings. That includes:

• Your Target Company List. Remember you're going to ask things like, "Do you know anything about this or that company? What's the best way to approach them? Can you recommend anyone I can talk to there like we're doing here today?"

• Being very clear on who you are meeting, what you know about the person, and how you were referred. You'll be seeing lots of people and it's easy to get confused about who said what and who does what. Think how embarrassing it would be if you mention that "Joel Zigler speaks highly of you" when it was actually Phoebe Phennign who sent you to this person. Review your notes before each meeting.

• Articles about particular companies you want information

on. In this situation, you'll be showing someone the article and asking if they know more about this company or the president or so-and-so who's quoted in the article.

• Your good looks and character. Even though you're not going into these meetings with the goal to be offered a position, you want to show your best side. So always, always, always present yourself in the best possible light. Act and dress the same way you would in any business meeting.

• A well-thought-out response to possible objections. If you're prepared to handle someone's concerns about your move or the type of position you want, you won't be thrown if you hear them. You'll be more relaxed, professional, and make a better impression.

• A goal of what you want to leave with. Before you go into each meeting, review what you want to come out of it with. What specific information do you want? What particular referrals would be helpful?

Most of this is information neatly organized in your Move Manifesto.

Now let's talk about situations and opportunities that could pop up while you're in these meetings or afterwards and what to do next. The possibilities are:

◆ YOU GET GREAT REFERRALS

This is something you counted on. So now what do you do since you only have between four and ten days in which to meet these new people you've been referred to?

Simple. Pick up the phone, share the purpose of your call, who referred you, and the fact that you're only here for the week. (Here's where that phone script comes in handy.) Under the circumstances, I have found most people willing to meet on short notice, but not everyone will or can. If they are willing, set a time and date and get directions. If there's time and it makes sense, do a little research on the company and, possibly, your referral.

If someone is hesitant to meet or is short on time and you really want to meet, offer to take the person to lunch or breakfast. Everybody has to eat. As a last resort, talk on the phone.

◆ YOU LEARN OF AN OPENING

If someone tells you they know so-and-so is looking for someone just like you, do whatever you can to get an interview.

If your contact knows the person, see if he or she would be willing to call their associate and give them the heads-up by saying something like, "Just wanted to let you know, I met Lolita Lycus who's visiting here from Minneapolis. She's got great credentials for that sales position you have open. I told her to call you, so expect her call."

When you make the call, be sure to reference the person you both know to jog your new contact's memory. *Do not assume* your new contact will remember who you are, even if they only hung up with their associate an hour ago. People are so busy, they go from one thing to the next, and forget about what they were just dealing with. Your job search is a priority for you only.

If someone tells you about a position but doesn't know anyone at the company, find out who would be responsible for the hiring of the position (not the human resource person, but the manager or supervisor the position reports to). Call this person and tell him or her how you heard about the position, that you're in town just this week, and ask if you can set up an interview.

The same applies if you learn of a position through any other source. When one of my clients was visiting his target market he read an article in the newspaper about the fact that the general manager of a radio station was leaving. He applied for the job while he was there and several interviews and months later was offered the job.

◆ A MEETING SHIFTS INTO AN INTERVIEW

If you're sitting there talking about your career objective and qualifications and the person begins to ask probing questions, pay close attention. You could be under consideration for a job at their company.

Is he delving into more detail about your knowledge, asking about your salary requirements, or how long it would be before you move there? These could be signs that the nature of your meeting has changed. When you hear these types of questions and sense something's up, you can give a response, then add, "I'm curious, why do you ask?"

If your meeting has gone way over a half an hour, there might be a reason. If there's no apparent reason for him to be giving you a tour of the business—but he does—something could be up. On the other hand, the person might just want to talk or is really proud of the company and wants to show you around.

He could just come out and say, "We do have an opening for someone with your qualifications."

If your informational meeting has turned into a job interview, go with the flow. Start thinking about questions you want to ask that will help you decide if you want to consider a job at this company.

Find out where the company is headed and why. Get a better understanding of the organization and its relationship to any subsidiaries. Show your interviewer you are interested in the overall company strategy and how you can contribute to it. Questions might include:

- What are the long-term goals of your company?
- Who are your competitors?
- What's the biggest issue facing your company?
- What kind of technology does the company use?

Really check out the company. You don't want to make a geographical move to a firm that is not well run or positioned for future success.

Besides the company, check out the position. Ask about:

- Specific responsibilities of the job and challenges the division or department faces
- Why the position is open
- What a typical day in this job would be like
- Who you'd report to
- How your responsibilities would be evaluated
- What it is about you and your background that leads them to think you might be a fit

Ask to see a job description. If they don't have one, check out a book like *The Big Book of Jobs* (VGM), *The O*Net Dictionary of Occupational Titles* (JIST), or the *Dictionary of Occupational Titles* (VGM).

Investigate the company culture and leadership by asking about:

- How the company supports the development of employees
- What kind of infrastructure the company has to be able to be customer-focused
- Performance reviews—are they given regularly? What criteria are they based on?
- If mentoring and coaching is encouraged
- How management communicates to employees

- Team efforts, risk-taking, and creativity, and whether they are encouraged and rewarded

By the way, these questions I mention here are ones you can also ask in a meeting that was initially set as a job interview. But you may have already done some of this research, knowing you were going to explore a possible match between you and the company.

Since this might be your big chance to find out as much information as you can, use it. If it feels right, ask to meet with other people in the organization.

If you're asked to go through a more formal interview process with the human resource folks, do whatever they ask. One of my clients who is a seasoned executive said, "Filling out an application with the human resources people seemed bogus as hell. I hadn't done that in a long time and it reminded me of applying to Arby's as a fifteen-year-old. Nonetheless, I smiled and filled it out."

At the end of your meeting, get a clear understanding of what's next. Do they feel you're a good match? Where are they in the process? Are they still interviewing? Be sure to set up your next step. Do they want references? Will they be getting back to you? If so, when?

No matter how well things go, though, please don't go ape over an offer if you get one (which is highly unlikely this early in the game) and make any hasty decisions while you're there. Wait at least until you get back home and you're more objective. Tell the interviewer that you're very interested in the position and why. Explain that you need time to evaluate it. You were, after all, here just to gather information. However, you're excited about this opportunity, but you do need time to sort everything out. In Chapter 7, I'll talk about how to evaluate job offers.

You may not feel at all prepared to make such a decision this early in the process, but you still don't want to shut any doors.

When you get home, you can call the company and explain where your head is. Who knows where that will be until you get through this phase.

One more thing: Even if you think this is the greatest job since sliced bread, go to the other meetings you have planned while you're there. For one, you can get more information on this company in those meetings. And two, you might discover other positions—even a better one. Continue to check out other known openings. More information will help you know if this one is as good as it seems.

◆ YOU CAN CREATE A POSITION

I have had clients go into meetings in which they were totally focused on getting advice and information and come out with a job offer for a position that didn't even exist. Now this situation is different from the one I just talked about—an offer for a position that *already* exists.

How does this happen? Well, for one thing, these clients were darn good at talking about themselves and demonstrating their value. They developed a good rapport, presented themselves as effective communicators, were confident about their skills, and showed how effective they'd been in the past.

If they were talking to a company in their industry, they had done their homework and knew what the needs and problems of such a company were and how their expertise could help. They asked intelligent, insightful questions during the conversation.

They never crossed the line of what they said they were there for in the first place. It wasn't until the person they were talking to brought up the subject of a possible position that the nature of the discussion changed. Even then, they were cautious.

The clues? The conversation suddenly switched to something like this:

HEAD HONCHO: Mmmm, that's very impressive that you were able to get your company into a global market like that. So, do you think you could do something like that at a company like ours?

or:

HEAD HONCHO: You know we've never done anything like that here. But it's something I've been thinking about for a while. I know we need to do it. Maybe the time is right to bring someone like you on board and create this department.

What if this happens to you? Creating a new position and everything that goes with it takes time. But you've got their attention. If you're interested, keep the conversation going. Explore this together. Ask open-ended questions like, "Tell me more about what you're thinking . . ." or "How would you see something like this happening?"

After you've discussed the idea and how you could be involved, share your interest in exploring the possibilities further. Ask other open-ended questions like: "How do you think we should proceed?"

The most logical approach is for you to come back with a proposal. I'm not suggesting you spend hours developing detailed marketing plans, competitive analysis, specific strategies, budgets—that sort of thing. That's something you would get paid to do.

A woman once wrote me that she was a finalist for a job and had been asked to write a marketing plan. The company was not only picking her brain for free, but it was taking advantage of the vulnerable position she already felt she was in. She really wanted the job and thus was willing to do whatever the company asked.

That's not what I'm talking about when I suggest you develop a proposal. This type of proposal is an outline of the specific problems the newly created position would address. It's not necessarily a job description, although you might talk about some of the responsibilities. It's more of a description of the company's overall objective and how this position would contribute to that. You can list specific goals of the position and general ways you'd address them. Since the position hasn't really been hatched yet, developing this outline will help you and the employer understand the scope of the position, which will lead to the next discussion either in person or on the phone.

If you do get the go-ahead to explore a position, and plan to talk with the employer more, do not abandon your other job-search activities. Please read that sentence again. I can't emphasize this enough. Like I said before when we talked about meetings that turn into job interviews, keep your scheduled meetings. Try to set up more. Check out other openings. Go full force ahead as if this possible new position were never mentioned. The job may not ever pan out.

◆ YOU GET REFERRED TO HUMAN RESOURCES

Some well-meaning people might give you the name of a human resources professional to contact. If they do, they either (1) don't understand what you're trying to do, or (2) don't understand how people get hired. Therefore, don't get all that excited about getting these kinds of referrals.

Let me explain. Bless human resources people, but please understand that they do not hire or create jobs. They screen out people. If you get referred to a human resources person, you're basically getting the name of the person who gets résumés and decides whether to pass them on to the people who do know what and who they need (now or in the future) and have the power to hire. You could have gotten the human resources person's name in a directory or by calling the company. You didn't need a referral.

Instead, you want a referral to the person I just described—the vice president, director, president, manager, or supervisor—depending on the size of the company and your level.

If, however, you are in the field of human resources and get referrals to other professionals in your field, that is another story.

◆ GET INTO GOOD HABITS

At the end of every day, complete your Interview Record Forms if you haven't done them during the day. Make any calls to confirm other meetings and write thank-you notes. Have a nice dinner.

Call home from time to time and reconnect with the people you care about. When you're on strange turf, it can get lonely. Keep them updated. Ask for encouragement if you need it. Then get a good night's sleep.

WHEN THINGS AREN'T GOING WELL

It is possible that you will run into dead ends. Either you don't get good information or no one wants to refer you to anyone. You're not going to like what I'm about to say, but, this is most likely more a reflection of what you are or aren't doing than anything else.

For example, let's say you're not getting much or any information. Odds are you're probably not asking good questions. Or you're expecting others to know what you should be asking them.

If you're not getting referrals, you're probably not doing the first four steps of the meeting well. Whenever someone tells me they got nowhere in their meetings, a conversation similar to this one ensues:

ME: So how did your meetings go, Dick?

DICK: Not very good. I didn't learn anything I didn't already know.

ME: Tell me about your meetings.

DICK: Well, I did everything you said. I told people about myself, I gave my three-minute commercial. And then I asked questions.

ME: What specifically did you ask?

DICK: I asked the first six people I met with, "What can you tell me that will help me find a job here?" That kind of thing.

ME: Mmmm. I don't remember suggesting that as a question.

DICK: Well, it just seemed like a good way to get to the point. People are busy, you know. Then when I didn't get anywhere I just started asking them who they knew that I could talk to. They said they'd have to think about it.

ME: And I'm assuming you didn't get any referrals?

DICK: Not a one. People were not helpful at all.

Duh (I wanted to say that to him). But being the nice person that I am, I said: "I'm not surprised."

People like Dick who don't get results give up on the process without ever trying it. Then they say the process doesn't work.

Obviously, the response Dick got (or lack of it) was a polite way to get rid of him. He didn't do any of the things he was supposed to do:

1. Think through *specific* questions each person could potentially help him with, depending on who they are and how his own referral felt they could help.
2. Get to know people, which would lead to them wanting to help him.

He made a big no-no asking people for referrals before the other person even had a chance to get to know him and want to help him and, therefore, refer him to their friends and colleagues.

It's obvious that Dick doesn't trust the process. Sure people are busy. But they agreed to meet with him, didn't they? He really wastes their time when he conducts the meeting the way he described. What he doesn't seem to understand is that he adds value to their life *and* his when he goes about it the right way.

I can't be there with you in your meetings. So it's up to you to be honest with yourself and really look at what you're saying and doing in these meetings. I can tell you this though: If you work the process, the process works.

ANOTHER THING TO WATCH FOR

The way you communicate is critical here. Even if you're in a high-tech business, communication skills are very important. People will be making judgments about you based on how you communicate. These people—your conduit to employers or perhaps to jobs in their companies—want to hear someone who can express ideas clearly, articulate their goals, and answer questions in a way that's easy to understand.

This is especially important if you're a recent college graduate. Since you won't have a lot of experience, you will be judged on your potential and your ability to build relationships and present yourself.

IN YOUR SPARE TIME

In between meetings, you can set up other meetings with the people you get referred to, conduct research, and write thank-you letters—which I've talked about before. Besides that:

• Follow up with people you met with.

If you really connected with someone, they were especially helpful and said to be sure and keep in touch, it can't hurt to touch base during the week just to say how things are going. If you're running into any problems or need a recommendation for something, this is the type of person to call.

• Learn about openings.

Read the news and wants ads in the daily paper (remember my client who read a news story about the fact that the general manager of a radio station was leaving?) Attend a local job focus group if you know of one. Keep your eyes open for places and publications that have job listings. If you discover anything interesting, telephone the appropriate person, tell him or her you're in town this week and would like to set up an interview.

• Pull out your Move Manifesto, look over your reason-for-moving statement, and ask yourself: Can I achieve that here? Look at your checklist of "What's Important to Me." Does this place have that? Check out the things that are on that list.

HONEST-TO-GOODNESS JOB INTERVIEWS

The same parameters apply to a job interview out of town as they do to one in your hometown. In a first interview, your goal is to present yourself in the best possible light, learn as much as you can about the position, and decide if it's a good fit. If you decide it is, your goal is to get invited to the second interview.

The company's goal is to decide whether you're a good fit. Before you were invited in, a couple of people decided from looking at your résumé and cover letter that you had the basic technical skills and education they needed—in other words, you could do the job.

Now they want to see if you have the right attitude and work ethic, that you can handle setbacks, are willing to learn, are self-motivated and honest. They're looking at first impressions and how you'd fit in with Beth and Morry and Steve and Susan and the rest of the team.

If you get to a second round while you're in town, you'll probably meet with other people at the company. Now find out in greater detail what they're looking for, share your interest in the position, and always know where you stand before you leave. Ask, "Where do we go from here?"

As soon as you can, type a thank-you note to everyone you met with. This is not only the courteous thing to do, but it echoes your interest.

Tip: Remember that you may be head over heels about the position and ready to go for it. But back at the farm, other things could be brewing. A week after everything about the position looked rosy, the company could scrap the job. They could have lost the new business this position was going to handle. Or a new president may have taken over and put a hold on hiring. The company may have been acquired. The person who interviewed you could have left the company. The position could have completely changed and your skills no longer fit what they need.

You never know what's going on behind closed doors, so even though you're raring to go, the company may not be working in your time frame. That's another reason you don't put all of your eggs in one basket.

WHEN YOU'RE ANTSY TO MOVE

Now that you're in the place you really want to be, you might decide not to be as methodical about this approach as I'd like you to be. In other words, you're hell bent on moving, even without a job.

If you go through this first trip (or you've been there several times before) and decide, "This is where I want to be and I'm moving, that's all there is to it," fine. It's not the best approach for most people, but, hey, it could be what's right for you. So if you're determined to move now, let's talk about ways to get some money in your pocket—temporarily anyway—and where else to focus your attention on this first trip.

Margie was a client of mine who decided she was moving to Arizona come hell or high water.

"My husband had been saying since our marriage, 'Within five years, we'll be living in Arizona.' Well, five years came and went and with each passing year, he said the same thing," she related.

"I finally told him that the five-year plan wasn't working and that we needed to just go and check it out. We flew there to look around and see if we'd like living there. We drove around with a realtor and after about four days my husband said, 'I think we have different expectations for this trip. You seem to be looking for a house. I thought we were just trying to see if we like the place and can afford it. Then we'd come back another time to look for a house.' He was right, so I agreed to hold off on the house hunting." But Margie was eager to move and eventually they moved, although only one of them had secured a job.

If you want to consider moving without a firm offer, here are some things to do while you're on this trip:

◆ Explore Optional Working Arrangements

Temping

This can be a good route to take if you're moving no matter what or if you're a trailing partner or spouse and you're also moving, no matter what. It's also a way to test the market.

Temporary work offers you flexibility, mobility, and the chance to see what's available at a company. And it can lead to a permanent job. You might work in a place, decide you don't like it, and not go back. You can work in different companies. Check out Interim Services (www.interim.com), which has a large pool of temporary and flexible-time positions. They recruit on the Internet.

Margie registered with a temporary agency that kept her working 50 percent of the time. Meanwhile, she looked for a full-time job. During that five-month period she was offered five different positions.

Lyna, a teacher, got her full-time job through a temporary position. On her first visit to her targeted market, she went to four county offices to find a substitute teaching job. During the next two months, she was offered a long-term substitute job to fill in for a teacher on pregnancy leave. She took it, moved, and the position lead to a full-time job in that school.

Benny decided to move to Atlanta, although he didn't have a job waiting. He was in TV broadcasting and production and living in Edmonton, Alberta, where he had gone to work for a company that was building a new television station and production facility. After four winters there, he and his family decided they were ready to head back south.

He made several visits to Atlanta before moving, "going around with my newly printed business cards and videotape demo reels under my arm." He got to know people through one-on-one meetings. After he moved he joined a no-league softball team. He also worked part-time for his father-in-law building homes, while doing freelance TV and film production work and pursuing full-time jobs.

"I traded a good-paying management job for an hourly construction one." But he knew it was temporary. Eventually he got a management job at Turner Broadcasting.

If you know from the get-go that you're moving even without a position, you can tell people this—which could open up some possibilities. For instance, if you and a company really hit it off, but they're not ready to look at a full-time position, maybe a part-time one would be an option. Bring it up as a possibility.

Even if you're not quite ready to move, you might want to talk to a temporary agency or local recruiter and let them know you're available.

Internships

Many people—especially recent college graduates—take internships that pay little or sometimes nothing at all to be at a company or location of their choice. There's no guarantee, but this is another way you can move with a possibility of a full-time job down the road.

◆ **GET IN A LITTLE SIGHTSEEING AND VISITING**

If you gave yourself time to check out the area, here are some things to add to your itinerary:

• Meet with a realtor

Besides driving around to see the community, be sure to get a relocation packet from the realtor. This is a big package of information that will tell you about neighborhoods, parks, art and entertainment, schools, restaurants, museums, libraries, sports, shopping, hospitals, and places of worship. Attend some open houses in neighborhoods you like.

Make sure you work with a realtor you like. One of my clients used the realtor his new boss had recommended, which he says, "May have been politically correct, but that's about it." Meet with several different ones before you decide to work with one. Besides being comfortable with the person, they should be familiar with the parts of town you're interested in.

• If you have children, check out recreational activities, library services, child-care options, and schools. When it comes to schools, according to the Employee Relocation Council, here's what to evaluate:

School's budget history

Accreditation

Mean SAT scores and how they compare to neighboring schools

Student/teacher ratios

Percentage of students graduating

Gifted programs and accelerated or advanced study

Availability of special programs such as music, art, drama, and foreign language

Student support services, such as psychologists, speech and hearing therapists, counselors, and services for the disabled.

If you have high-school-aged children you may want to visit area college campuses.

Later on, when you decide where you'll land, it can be helpful to include kids in a home-buying trip so they can see the neighborhoods.

• Visit places. Thoroughly check out the spots that will add joy to your life. One man who was considering a move from Chicago to a smaller Midwestern city wanted to make sure there was an active Jewish community in the city, so he visited the Jewish Center and attended a social event to get more insight into that area of his life that was very important to him. He also went to a benefit party for Big Brothers/Big Sisters, where he met people and got a better feel for the community.

There's nothing like seeing a place and the people in it first hand.

TAKE ADVANTAGE OF EVERY MOMENT

Layovers are a possibility, so if you are on your way to or from your destination and have a layover at the airport, take advantage of it. Some airports have a service called Laptop Lane, which allows travelers to rent office space for a short time. You can use a phone, fax, print information, even use the net.

WHEN IT'S ALL SAID AND DONE

People use many different terms to describe this part of the process: hard, frustrating, hopeful, insightful, and wonderful. Most of my clients come back to town exhilarated. They've met new people, discovered possibilities they didn't know existed, and had meetings they never anticipated.

Go with realistic expectations, work the process, and come back to town prepared to work the process some more.

6

HOW TO BE A NICE NAG

This is not going to be sexy. Now that you're back from an action-packed week or two talking to people and discovering a new place, get ready for the grunge work—the nuts and bolts of follow-up. You gotta do it. Otherwise your trip will have been for naught.

Before I get into that, be prepared for a reaction you might have upon your return from this trip: The "Was it worth it?" reaction.

See, you left on a mission and so you'll come back with an expectation that you accomplished what you set out to do. You'll question whether the trip was worth it. You'll whip out the calculator to add up your expenses and justify the cost and time you spent being away. And you'll get yourself in a heap of trouble.

Remember in Chapter 4 how we talked about your goals and what to expect before you left? How you're not expecting to come back with a job? How that's simply not realistic or something you're ready for yet?

But no matter how much I nudge you about it, you may not listen. Admit it, in the back of your mind you're thinking maybe, just maybe, someone *will* offer me a fabulous job on this first trip. If you expect that to happen, you'll be disappointed in the results of the trip. You'll think you're a failure and mope around for days cursing yourself: "I knew this would never work."

On the other hand, if you're realistic (something I firmly believe in if you're going to get anywhere in this world) you'll be delighted with the results, which I'll talk about in a minute. First, one more thing to be aware of upon your return home.

Besides thirsty plants, expect to be greeted with messages on your phone machine and e-mail from friends and family. Messages that go something like this:

"So, what happened? Did you get a job? When are you moving? Was it worth it? Call me . . . I'm dying to know how it went."

To help cope with the anxiety you might be feeling from your own expectations and well-meaning friends and family, now is the time to take stock of your trip.

SIZE UP WHAT YOU ACCOMPLISHED

Remember, the object of your trip was to:

1. Get information about the community, industries and companies
2. Meet new people and get them to know you, like you and want to help you
3. Hold meetings with people to gather information and feedback and, if possible, have job interviews
4. Weave your way into the community and penetrate the job market
5. Get a better idea of how you like the area as a place to live and work

If you did all that, then you:

Made inroads into a new community. Before you left you were a total stranger to everyone there, right? But look at you now. You know ten, twenty, thirty, or more new people. Everybody from the neighborhood dry cleaner who you swapped apple pie recipes with to the CEO of a company. And that's just the beginning.

You've begun to build credibility with people in the community. You met people who have jobs and know other people and can therefore introduce you to the people they know. Some people did. And that, you'll recall from my bludgeoning you over the head fourteen times in earlier chapters, is the best way to discover opportunities.

Saw firsthand what the place was like. If you'd never been there before, now you have a picture of it. You can be more realistic about what the place is like. A dose of reality is good.

Got a better feel for the types of industries and companies and what they're like. Even if you had a list of companies and industries beforehand, you couldn't really know what they are like. But now you've walked into the businesses and driven around the area. You've got a sense of their culture and environment. You may have even decided to cross some off your list. Now you can be more strategic about whom to target. That's using the old noggin.

Got a strong indication of where you fit into this market. You talked to people in businesses about yourself and their needs. You know more about how they perceive you, and if and where you can create a job for yourself. This helps you know how to position yourself. Good work.

Are more likely to be considered for job openings. Instead of just a voice on the phone or name on a résumé, you're a real live breathing, walking, talking human being who came all the way there to find out more about the community. You have demonstrated your commitment. This will double your odds of being considered for openings. You made major points.

Gathered information that helps you decide your next move. Doing all of the above helps you know how to refine your strategy to get you closer to your next position. Nice going.

All of this makes for a strong foundation for a job search in a new place. You did a great job. Pat yourself on the back. In fact, treat yourself to a nice dinner out. There's probably nothing worth eating in the refrigerator, anyhow.

So as you can see, even if you didn't come home with a job

offer—or one you wanted—you succeeded. A job offer wasn't your goal.

Please do keep family and friends updated. Remind them of your objective. You'll be tempted to say: "Would you just leave me alone. I'm doing everything I can. I'm reading this book and doing everything it tells me to. Just stop bugging me!"

Don't. You need all the support you can get. Instead, try something like:

"I really appreciate your interest in my job search. I'm taking a very strategic approach. This trip was the first part of my plan. I accomplished and learned a lot, met many people, and now I'm working on the next part. I'll keep you updated." That should take care of things.

Now let's talk about how to reinforce what you accomplished, build momentum, and decide on your next steps.

WHAT DOES YOUR GUT SAY?

◆ EVALUATE HOW YOU FEEL ABOUT THE PLACE

Whether you had been there five times or never before, on this trip you went with a different perspective. Can you picture yourself living there? Making a living there? Did the community feel like home? Did you like the people? Did the area offer what you want in terms of culture, climate, activities, environment, education? How did you feel when you got off the plane or drove into town and sensed the place?

This gut check can have great impact on your decision to move to a new location. What if the place wasn't anything like you thought? Or isn't a place where you can earn a living? Could be time for Plan B.

One of my clients, Fay—who was in advertising—was considering a move to Santa Fe, New Mexico. She had been there on vacation and fell in love with the area. But once she revisited the state and looked at it from a career perspective, she had to reevaluate her plan. Santa Fe is not exactly the advertising mecca of America. If she wanted to work in an agency setting, she needed to look at the only large city in the state—Albuquerque.

There was only one large agency there where she could build her portfolio, so her options were limited. She interviewed at this agency and thought about her future there. When she was honest with herself she realized she really didn't want to live in Albuquerque. It would defeat one of her goals, to move to a more remote, less congested area. Her other goal was to eventually be in a career more closely related to fine art.

So after her visit, she considered Plan B—a complete career change. She weighed the pros and cons of moving to Santa Fe. Here, she could pursue her interest in art by working for one of the many art galleries. More risky? Perhaps. But she decided if she was going to make a move, it was going to be for something she wanted. She opted for Plan B.

If, on the other hand, you're a trailing partner, Plan B may not be an option.

WHAT DOES YOUR HEAD SAY?

◆ ORGANIZE YOUR RESEARCH

Sit down with all the data and impressions you gathered and organize them so you can objectively evaluate them. This is where your "What's Important to Me" Worksheet from Chapter 1 comes in. Now is the time to sit down and compare what you said you wanted with what you saw on your visit. I've created some forms for you to use to organize this data as well as other information you gathered into eight areas: overall community, industries, companies, people, positions uncovered, positions you could create, positions you want, and what you need more information on.

Before you get to the forms, look through the following questions I've listed for each of these areas to get you thinking about what you experienced.

◆ OVERALL COMMUNITY

People
Are they friendly, conservative, open-minded, health-conscious, nosy, professional, well-educated, diverse?

Physical Environment
Is it urban, rural, high-traffic, noisy, polluted, remote? Are the buildings new or deteriorating? Do they get tornadoes, earthquakes, or hurricanes?

Other Environment
Is it family-oriented, business-oriented, small-town, big-city, provincial, conservative, laid-back, entrepreneurial?

Cost of Living
What are the taxes and costs for housing, transportation, food, and recreation?

Commute
What is the area's transportation system like? Do you need a car to get around? Is it close to an airport? What's a typical commute time?

Health Care
Are there hospitals, specialty physicians, and clinics nearby? How many?

Crime Rate

How many police and firefighters are there? What are the crime statistics?

Education

What's the quality of education? Is there easy access to schools? How much priority is put on education?

Social and Cultural Life

Are there art exhibits, symphonies, theaters, museums, and international-cuisine restaurants? Is there close proximity to a university?

Recreation

What sports are available? Are there professional teams? Can you ski, camp, or hike?

Climate and Landscape

Is it hot, cold, humid, sunny, gray, windy, snowy, damp, dry, or rainy there? Are there deserts, mountains, an ocean, lakes, grass, open spaces?

Business Climate

Is business in a growth mode, slow, steady, diverse? Are there many small businesses?

◆ INDUSTRIES

Which of the manufacturers or service industries, such as banks and insurance, retail, farming, high-tech, and universities, are growing? Which ones do you fit into?

◆ COMPANIES

Which ones could use your expertise? Which ones would you like to work for? Which ones wouldn't you want to work for in a million years? Which ones do you need more information on?

◆ PEOPLE

Who did you talk to? (The details of what you learned from each person go on the Meeting Record Form we discussed in Chapter 4.) Who do you still want to talk to?

◆ POSITIONS UNCOVERED

What are they? What are the names of the companies? Who are your contacts?

◆ POSITIONS YOU COULD CREATE

What are they and where are they? Who's your contact?

◆ WHAT YOU NEED MORE INFO ON

Did you learn a little about a particular industry or company but want to know more? Who can you call and what do you want to ask? Where can you research information?

Fill in this information on the Round 1 Evaluation Worksheets on the following pages.

Round 1 Evaluation Worksheet 1

Overall Community

People: _____

_____

Physical environment: _____

_____

Other environment: _____

_____

Cost of living: _____

_____

Commute: _____

_____

Health care: _____

_____

Crime rate: _____

_____

Education: _____

_____

Social and cultural life: _____

_____

Recreation: _____

_____

Climate and landscape: _____

_____

Business climate: _____

_____

Round 1 Evaluation Worksheet 2

Industries in Area

Types

Ones that are growing

1. _____
   _____
2. _____
   _____
3. _____
   _____
4. _____
   _____
5. _____
   _____
6. _____
   _____
7. _____
   _____

Ones I fit into

1. _____
   _____
2. _____
   _____
3. _____
   _____
4. _____
   _____
5. _____
   _____
6. _____
   _____
7. _____
   _____

Companies in Those Industries

Specific names

1. _____
   _____
2. _____
   _____
3. _____
   _____
4. _____
   _____

Ones that could
use my expertise

1. _____
   _____
2. _____
   _____
3. _____
   _____
4. _____
   _____

Ones I'd like to
work for

1. _____
   _____
2. _____
   _____
3. _____
   _____
4. _____
   _____

Round 1 Evaluation Worksheet 2, continued

5. _____   5. _____   5. _____
   _____   _____   _____

6. _____   6. _____   6. _____
   _____   _____   _____

7. _____   7. _____   7. _____
   _____   _____   _____

8. _____   8. _____   8. _____
   _____   _____   _____

9. _____   9. _____   9. _____
   _____   _____   _____

10. _____   10. _____   10. _____
    _____   _____   _____

Ones I wouldn't work for in a million years: _____
_____
_____

Companies I need more information on: _____
_____
_____

Next step: _____
_____
_____

Round 1 Evaluation Worksheet 3

People

Who I talked to

1. _____
   _____
2. _____
   _____
3. _____
   _____
4. _____
   _____
5. _____
   _____
6. _____
   _____
7. _____
   _____
8. _____
   _____
9. _____
   _____
10. _____
    _____
11. _____
    _____
12. _____
    _____

Next step

1. _____
   _____
2. _____
   _____
3. _____
   _____
4. _____
   _____
5. _____
   _____
6. _____
   _____
7. _____
   _____
8. _____
   _____
9. _____
   _____
10. _____
    _____
11. _____
    _____
12. _____
    _____

Round 1 Evaluation Worksheet 3, continued

Who I want to talk to	Next step
1. _____	1. _____
_____	_____
2. _____	2. _____
_____	_____
3. _____	3. _____
_____	_____
4. _____	4. _____
_____	_____
5. _____	5. _____
_____	_____
6. _____	6. _____
_____	_____
7. _____	7. _____
_____	_____
8. _____	8. _____
_____	_____

Round 1 Evaluation Worksheet 4
(Copy this for each position)

Position I Uncovered

Position: _____

_____

_____

_____

_____

_____

Company: _____

_____

_____

_____

_____

_____

Contact: _____

_____

_____

_____

_____

_____

Next step: _____

_____

_____

_____

_____

Round 1 Evaluation Worksheet 5
(Copy this for each position)

Position I Could Create

Position: _____
_____
_____
_____
_____
_____

Company: _____
_____
_____
_____
_____
_____

Contact: _____
_____
_____
_____
_____
_____

Next step: _____
_____
_____
_____
_____
_____

Round 1 Evaluation Worksheet 6

What I Need More Information on

Subject: _____

_____

_____

_____

_____

_____

_____

_____

Who to call and what to ask: _____

_____

_____

_____

_____

_____

_____

_____

What publications to read; web site to check out: _____

_____

_____

_____

_____

_____

_____

Any place you wrote "I need more information" start digging. Either use the contacts you just made or other resources, such as annual reports, chambers of commerce, books from the library and bookstore, or the Internet. Concentrate on the Next Steps that you wrote on Worksheets 2 and 3. The following will help you know how to take those steps and get successful results.

You'll find six scenarios that could happen on your visit. First I outline the scenario, then I describe the follow-up action to take.

FOLLOW-UP

◆ SITUATION A

You'd like to work for Company A. You met someone there who's seriously interested in having you be part of their organization but there are no openings right now.

Action

Keep in regular contact. Anything could happen. The person who's in the job you'd be perfect for could give their two weeks' notice tomorrow. Your contact may have been so bowled over by you, she finds a way to get rid of that person.

First write a thank-you letter to your contact (check the business card you received so that you use the correct spelling and title). See Sample Letter A at the end of this chapter.

This letter keeps the door open for you to call or write back. So do exactly that. Mark on your calendar when you're following up (in two to four weeks—depending on how you left things). This is when you'll check back to tell them how your search is going and if and when you'll be back in town and to snoop around to see if anything has changed at their company. (More details in a minute.) Tell them you'll keep in contact.

◆ Situation B

You met someone from Company B who seems interested in you, but you:

1. wouldn't want to work for them in a million years
2. didn't find anything they said to be helpful

Action

Whether it was an informational meeting or an interview for a potential job opening, write a nice letter to this person to thank him or her for the meeting you found utterly useless. (Don't tell them that.) It's a small world. And even if you have no interest in working for their company or them, this individual is still a part of your network and may be able to refer you to someone or give you information on something else you need later. Besides, it's the right thing to do. See Sample Letter B.

◆ Situation C

You discover Company C—a place you think you'd like to work (or at least have the opportunity to talk to someone there to find out) but didn't meet with anyone from there on this trip. For example, let's say you're on the plane headed home and you read about a new software developer. The place sounds fabulous. They're progressive and innovative. They specialize in multimedia marketing services and publish college search software. The article quotes the president, who discusses how much the company will be growing over the next three years.

Action

If you don't know anyone at the company but you met someone who might be able to introduce you to a decision maker there, share that in your thank-you letter with your contact. See Sample

Letter C1. Or write the president directly. Yeah, you heard right. What's the worst that can happen? See Sample Letter C2.

◆ Situation D

You discovered an opening at Company D and had an interview. No offer was made but you're interested.

Action

Write a thank-you letter which outlines the main points covered in your interview. See Sample Letter D. This letter can include a proposal, as I discussed in Chapter 5. This is an overview of what you would do in the position, highlighting the company's objective, and how you would help them meet their objective.

◆ Situation E

In your meeting with someone at Company E, you discovered a way to create a position for yourself. The two of you discussed this possibility. There's definite interest. You would also have talked about the next step.

Action

Write a thank-you letter, emphasizing what you discussed. The content of this letter also depends on the next step you agreed on. This is usually another appropriate time to write a proposal. In fact, if the discussion was serious, before you left the meeting you would have told your contact you'll be following up with a proposal to explore the position further. See Sample Letter E.

◆ SITUATION F

You met with someone purely for an informational meeting at Company F. You learned a lot from the discussion and you want to keep in contact.

Action

Send a thank-you letter. See Sample Letter F. Any follow-up you do after that will depend on how helpful you think this person can be and the relationship you established. If she was supposed to get more information for you—such as names and addresses—follow up when she said she'd have it.

Expect this initial round of thank-you letters and proposals to take a good week or so to complete. Start this process within a day or two of returning home. Otherwise, you'll put it off until the next day, and the next day will come and go. You'll have every intention of sending them out over the weekend, but something will come up. By now a week will have passed—maybe longer since some of your meetings were at the beginning of your visit. Add in the time it takes the post office to deliver your letters (my experience has been from two days to a month) and your contact will have forgotten all about you. Your trip will have been wasted.

THEN WHAT?

Your next step will depend on (1) what happened on the trip, (2) your finances, (3) your flexibility. One thing is certain: By now, you'll be ready to follow up with people you wrote and told you'd be in contact with in two to three weeks. Do it. Your reputation and credibility depend on it.

What's the big deal? Well, odds are they won't be thinking about you much if you don't connect quickly. But don't think they won't necessarily remember you told them you'd keep in contact. Or that they really don't want to hear from you. The majority of job hunters:

1. Don't follow up.
2. Don't write thank-you notes.
3. Aren't really interested in building relationships. They're just focused on solving their own problem—to get a job.

You will be noticed, remembered, and respected if you are different from everyone else.

"Credibility, like reputation, is something that is earned over time," say James Kouzes and Barry Posner in their book *Credibility*. You just started building your credibility with this new community. So don't mess up. It's simple if you follow the authors' prescription: DWYSYWD, which means: Do What You Say You Will Do. So if you said you'd call or write back in three weeks, do it. Got it? Besides, these people have invested their time in you and deserve a follow-up. Most people really do care.

◆ Reconnect by Letter, Phone, E-mail, or Fax

What if you have nothing new to report? Don't be ridiculous. Of course you do. Here are some of the reasons to follow up and what you have to say:

◆If you're reconnecting with someone from Company A (she's the one who's interested in having you on board but has no opening right now) or Company E (the company where you discovered a way to create a position for yourself) you can tell your contact things like:

The more I think about your company and the position, the more it seems like a good fit. Then remind her why:
In the research I've been doing on the net, I found out that

such and such a trend affects your company, which is all the more reason why you need someone with my expertise.

Send your contacts information they'd be interested in that could affect their work: studies, surveys, new data, referrals to people you know, and opportunities that will help them build their business—the one you want to be a part of. Don't let them forget you. Keep them thinking about you and that interest you generated on your trip. Remember, they need you. Otherwise the conversation wouldn't have gotten as far as it did.

If you plan to be back in the area, ask if you can meet for lunch. Your goal is to continue to build this relationship and show your interest.

◆Either call your contact who you wrote or the president you wrote at Company C (the one you think you'd like to work for). Your letter may have been passed on to someone else. That's fine. Talk to that person. Evaluate her interest in talking with you further.

Here's what your conversation might sound like:

YOU: Hello, this is Brad Osherwitz. I wrote Ms. Akea a letter two weeks ago in response to an article in the *Austin Business Journal.* I understand she passed that letter on to you?

MS. AKEA'S VP: Yes, I have it right here. She's out of town much of the time and asked me to follow up with you. So you're in marketing?

YOU: Yes, my career spans twelve years in marketing in which I worked for two very progressive start-ups that have become leaders in their industry.

VP: Well, how can I help you?

(This is where you need to know exactly what you want, which, in this case, is to meet when you're in town next month.)

YOU: As you can see from my letter, I'm moving to Austin by the end of the year and am exploring the area to learn more about the market and how I fit in. I thought it might make sense for us to meet. I know your company is growing and I'd like to learn more about your needs. And I'd also like to tell you more about myself. I think we probably have mutual interests."

VP: Well, why don't you and I set something up. What dates are you here?

I can't promise this is how every follow-up conversation will go, but if someone at a company sees potential in you and what you can do for them and they're smart, that could be the gist of how it will proceed.

◆If you haven't heard back from Company D (the one where you had a job interview), call them. Just as I described in Chapter 3, if the person you want to talk to isn't in, leave a message—no more than three times.

And in this case—or any others where you're following up— if people don't return your calls, try this. Go back to the person who referred you to the person you're trying to reach. Explain how unsuccessful you've been in getting in touch. Ask if she has any ideas on how to get through.

There's also another reason to do this—to protect your credibility. See, if the person who referred you thinks you didn't follow up on their suggestion (since they never heard anything more) they may think you're not reliable or serious about your career. This way they won't wonder if you ever followed up. A simple "Just wanted to let you know" will do.

◆If you told Company F (where you held an informational meeting) you'd follow up, do it by giving them an update of your activity. Tell him who else you talked to and why and if you'll be back in the area and when. This person may think of someone else you should talk to. He may have heard of an opening since you left. These periodic check-ins will keep you on this person's mind. You think he has nothing better to do than sit around and think about you? That's why you have to remind him.

What form should this contact take? If you said you'd call, call. If you just want to update someone (like Company F) you can write a letter. A letter doesn't interrupt someone the way a phone call does, it's professional, and tells the reader this is important because you took the time to write it, address it, and lick and stick a stamp on the envelope.

In any follow-up, consider your message and how this person likes to connect. Some people love e-mail. Others think it's impersonal. A 1997 survey conducted by Office Team found that most executives prefer face-to-face meetings best. E-mail was second best, paper memo was third favorite, and voice mail last.

Some people want to talk. Having a brief conversation with someone can really lift your spirits. It also gives someone the chance to react immediately. Play it by ear, depending on the person, the type of information you're conveying, what your goal is, and how soon you need a response. The more complex the information, the more I lean towards the written format. I only use faxes when someone says to send one or it's the only way to communicate.

◆ PLAN YOUR NEXT VISIT

If your schedule is flexible enough and you've budgeted for it, plan another trip there within two to six weeks or when there's an event you want to attend in the area.

Mickey was a client of mine who was committed to moving to Atlanta. She took one week's vacation for her first trip to the area. She planned her second trip for three weeks later, leaving on a Tuesday evening and returning on Sunday. Now she only had three days of vacation time left.

When the word got out to her boss that she was job hunting (she had told her colleague at work, which I warned her not to do), she decided to go on "special assignment." This is a very generous policy at her company that lets you ease out of your position while they pay you for up to twelve weeks as you look for a new job.

With her job hunt out in the open, she felt she had nothing to lose. Plus this action would give her the extra time she needed to visit the area. She ended up getting a new position within a month. To this day, though, I think she knew full well her colleague would leak the news. This may have been unconscious on her part, but knowing her and the situation, it helped force her to make a move she wanted but was scared to commit to. Okay, enough psychobabble. The point is, be honest with yourself about what you really want; otherwise, you can sabotage your efforts.

Most companies won't have this type of policy, so you will have to figure out how you can incorporate follow-up visits into your vacation, time off without pay, or even take a sabbatical.

What will you do during your second and third visits? The same type of things you did on your first trip, only this time you know people. You're showing everyone how serious you are about moving. You're more targeted and strategic because you have a better idea of who you want to talk to and possibly work for. You might have a list of six companies you know you want to talk to based on your new research. You can meet with people a second time. At the very least, talk to them on the phone. Again, you're reinforcing your commitment and doing what you said you would do.

You can go to professional meetings or a seminar that's scheduled that week. You might even plan your trip around the time of a meeting. For example, Mickey set up her second trip the week of an American Marketing Association luncheon so she could meet people.

OTHER OPTIONS

◆ A COMPANY BRINGS YOU IN FOR AN INTERVIEW

As you continue to talk to your first round of contacts and headhunters, and as you research the geographical area, search the Internet and read the local newspapers—you may discover an opening. This is one way to get a company to bring you to town for an interview. It's also possible that Company D will want to talk to you further and pay for your expenses this time. That would be nice, wouldn't it?

◆ HOLD MORE MEETINGS BY PHONE WITH PEOPLE YOU GET REFERRED TO

If it's not financially feasible or your schedule doesn't permit another trip right away, continue your job search via the telephone. Hold informational meetings with people whom your contacts refer you to and with the people those contacts refer you to. In the early planning stages we discussed in Chapter 4, you will have a rough idea of when you plan to be back in the area. So plan meetings accordingly.

Of course, you'll follow up with anyone you talk to with a thank-you letter and any other information you promise. Remember, your credibility is at stake here.

WHAT CAN HAPPEN NEXT?

◆ YOU GET A JOB OFFER

Congratulations. The next chapter tells you how to proceed.

◆ You Get an Offer, But It's Not the One You Want

I hesitate to say this, but depending on your situation, consider taking it—with caution. Reasons for accepting a job that you're not jumping for joy over include:

1. You feel pressured to get a job because your partner is moving soon or is already there. (First evaluate your finances to make sure it's absolutely necessary.)
2. You plan to move anyway and this would help you pay the bills until you can really dig into the community.

But please be wary of taking *anything* just to have a job. There's nothing worse than being in a new place—possibly by yourself—and hating your job. Only consider taking it if the job is something you won't develop migraine headaches and stomachaches over and it will meet your immediate goal. Don't look at it as a long-term position. It's a short-term solution. And plan to look for what you do want once you're a resident.

◆ Nothing Happens

You may not get any offers. Or it may take awhile for offers to hatch. A job search in your own city takes time. Expect a job search in another place to take longer. The more people you talk to, the more follow-up and research you do, and the better equipped you are to present yourself in a concise, enthusiastic way, the quicker you'll get results. It's just logical.

Warning: Do not put all of your eggs in one basket. I know I've said this before, but I can't tell you how important this is—so I'll say it again. Even if there's one very promising opportunity, keep investigating other options. I don't care how much you want it, how solid you think it is, how wonderful an opportunity it can be, don't depend on it. It may never happen.

One of my clients came back to town after a two-week visit in Oregon and said, "I've got three opportunities."

"Are they actual offers?" I asked.

"Well, not yet, but I'm sure they will be."

I pleaded with him to keep looking, not to count on these— especially since he hadn't even gotten an offer from any of them. Well, over the next month, at one of the companies he was *sure* he would get an offer, the vice president he talked to had left and no one else there had a clue as to what he was talking about. "Job? What job?" they all said.

The second company kept putting him off. We finally concluded the guy he met with was lying through his teeth when he said he wanted to hire him. The third company was bought by a competitor. So now a month had gone by, my client hadn't kept up his other activity and had to start from scratch. You could say he was bummed.

HANG TOUGH

About two months into Mickey's job search she began to get anxious. Here's how one of those antsy conversations went:

MICKEY: I've been to Atlanta twice. I should have gotten an offer by now.

ME: What makes you say that?

MICKEY: Well, I work for one of the leading consumer products manufacturers and have a lot of expertise to share. And people have met with me.

ME: So?

Silence. She hates when I say that.

MICKEY: The XYZ Company said they'd create a position for me.

ME: Uh-huh.

MICKEY: Why haven't they?

ME: How did you leave things with them?

She flips through her notes.

MICKEY: The owner of the company will be gone for two weeks, but the partner is interested.

ME: So how did you leave things? I asked again.

MICKEY: I will call the partner in two weeks after the owner is back.

ME: So it sounds like things are moving right along. And maybe after the two partners have talked and you've met with both of them and everyone feels comfortable, you'll get an offer . . . when the time is right.

It's not what she wanted to hear. But she needed to be reminded of reality. I also reminded her that another company that liked her had a lengthy internal system to go through when hiring from the outside. So she was waiting to hear back on that position. In another instance, a nonprofit organization had to present her proposal to its board, which didn't meet for another two weeks. An advertising agency was still conducting interviews. And two people she wanted to talk to were on vacation.

There is no such thing as when and how things "should" happen in this process. Like everything else in the world, your out-of-town job search will evolve one step at a time. And when people are good and ready and the time is right and the sun and the moon are aligned with Mars just so, you'll get an offer.

The problem is *you're* ready for something to happen now. Here are some ways to sustain yourself through this period of uncertainty:

◆ CONCENTRATE ON WHAT YOU CONTROL

Keep reminding yourself things are going on behind the scenes that you have no control over. So concentrate on what you do control. One is that tricky little mind of yours. Your tendency will be to read into things. For instance, if someone hasn't gotten back to you, you may start thinking: "They're not interested. They hate me. They never want to see my face again. They'd rather eat raw liver or drink poison than hire me."

Don't let your imagination get carried away like mine just did. It's fun, but potentially defeating. Until you know for sure where things stand, quit worrying.

You also control your activities. So write letters, follow up with people, and conduct more research.

◆ REMEMBER THAT THINGS HAPPEN IN STAGES

There's usually a first, second, third, even a fourth or fifth interview. Sometimes many people in an organization get involved in the decision making. Or the job they thought they needed to fill changes to something completely different. They may not even know what they want.

◆ KNOW THAT IF YOU DON'T GET A POSITION, IT DOESN'T MEAN THERE'S SOMETHING WRONG WITH YOU

For whatever reason, the company felt it wasn't a good match. Or there could be some internal political hocus-pocus going on. This is another one of those things you can't control. Move on and don't dwell on it. Look on the bright side: you can always ask the people at the company to refer you to other people they know.

◆ AT THE END OF EACH WEEK, REVIEW ALL THE GOOD THINGS THAT HAPPENED

Who did you talk to? What new information did you learn? What new opportunity arose? This is not some gloppy, positive-thinking thing I dreamed up. It really will renew you. And you'll probably be surprised to see how many positive things did happen and how much you accomplished.

◆ Stay Focused on Your Goal

Keep your goal and strategy that you developed in Chapter 2 posted on the wall in front of you. Reread your Move Mantra. Stick to the plan. Have faith that you'll get what you want. And, in good time, you will.

Situation A: You met someone who's interested in you but has no openings.

Sample Letter A

February 8, 1999

Mr. Ned Narlsky
Marketing Director
Mippin & Shmippin Company
7899 Ranch Road
Austin, TX 78734

Dear Mr. Narlsky:

Thank you for meeting with me when I was in Austin last week. The Tex-Mex restaurant you suggested for dinner was fabulous! I think I'm going to like it there.

Besides your good taste in restaurants, I was very impressed with how you developed the marketing program from the bottom up—not to mention the impact you had on sales.

I'm sure you could detect my enthusiasm and interest in being a part of your team. I've worked in two similar start-ups where I created and implemented long-range marketing plans that catapulted both firms into market leadership positions. This experience, as well as my successful track record in international trade, seem to be a perfect match to help your company meet its future global goals.

As I also shared, I am committed to moving to Austin by the end of this year. I'd like to keep you informed of my activities and stay updated on your needs. At this time, I plan to be back in your area from March 15 to 20. Perhaps I could take you to lunch. I will call early next week to see when lunch would be convenient.

Again, thank you for your time and hospitality.

Sincerely,

Brad Osherwitz

Situation B: You met someone who seems interested in you, but you're not interested in the company.

Sample Letter B

February 8, 1999

Ms. Rebecca Platoon
Marketing Manager
Reston Ridicule Manufacturing
28900 Congress Avenue
Austin, TX 78701

Dear Ms. Platoon:

I appreciated the opportunity to talk with you about the job market and Reston Ridicule Manufacturing when I was in Austin last week. Meeting Louis Cold and Janey Kaniption gave me a good sense of this industry and how I might fit in.

Your suggestion to meet Lucy Laboon was especially helpful and has already turned up some interesting opportunities. In the meantime I will continue to research other organizations that can use my marketing skills and background. I will keep you updated on my progress.

Thank you again for the chance to visit Reston Ridicule Manufacturing and for your hospitality.

Sincerely,

Brad Osherwitz

Situation C: You discover a place you think you'd like to work but don't know anyone there.

Sample Letter C1

February 8, 1999

Mr. Ollie Umphrey
Vice President
Steckel Advertising
4422 Klotz Way
Austin, TX 78701

Dear Mr. Umphrey:

Thank you again for meeting with me when I was in Austin last week. I appreciate all the time you took out of your busy morning. Having moved there yourself, you know how difficult it is to conduct a long-distance search. New acquaintances like you are a blessing.

Your suggestion to visit Littleburg Marketing and Research and the referral to Nancy Coopersmith were especially helpful. I'll let you know how that goes.

Remember the reading material you were so kind to give me? As I was wading through it on my flight home I read about a new software company that is starting up in your area. Are you familiar with Akeaware Inc.? Apparently, they specialize in multimedia marketing services and publish college search software. The article in the *Austin Business Journal* quoted Michelle Akea, the president, who discussed their planned growth over the next three years. Do you have any thoughts on the best way to approach them? The best way to reach me is by e-mail, or if you prefer, I've enclosed a self-addressed, stamped envelope.

In the meantime, I will keep you updated on my progress. Again, I can't thank you enough for your time and hospitality.

Sincerely,

Brad Osherwitz

Situation C: You discover a place you think you'd like to work but don't know anyone there.

Sample Letter C2

February 8, 1999

Ms. Michelle Akea
President
Akeaware Inc.
One Plaza Way
Austin, TX 78767

Dear Ms. Akea:

If you're looking for a creative and energetic marketer who can lead your company into the twenty-first century, we should talk.

I am currently exploring how to contribute my experience in innovative marketing and international trade to a progressive company in the Austin area. When I read about your vision to have a global presence by the twenty-first century, it seemed as if there might be a match between your needs and my expertise.

My qualifications include ten years working with two start-up firms where I created and implemented long-range marketing plans, catapulting both companies into market leadership positions. I also have a successful track record in international trade, helping both companies meet their global goals.

I am committed to moving to Austin by the end of this year, since my wife's company is relocating its headquarters in November. I will be back in the area March 15 and would like to meet to discuss a potential match between your needs and my qualifications. I will call early next week to see what date and time might be convenient.

Thank you.

Sincerely,

Brad Osherwitz

Situation D: You had an interview but no offer yet.

Sample Letter D

February 8, 1999

Mr. Filip Navidad
Managing Director
Kisch & Company
1131 Northwestern Avenue
Austin, TX 78767

Dear Mr. Navidad:

Thank you for the opportunity to meet and discuss the newly established Marketing Manager position. Talking to you and Anabelle Insepdido gave me a solid understanding of where your company wants to go and how my expertise can help you get there. In fact, the international market on which you want to focus is where I can be of immediate value.

I have successfully created and implemented global marketing strategies for two companies. As a result, both were catapulted to leading market positions, tripling their sales in the first six months. I have also led teams from five divisions to examine international growth opportunities that resulted in joint ventures in three emerging markets.

Everything I learned about your company and this position seem to be an excellent match with my qualifications and skills. I am excited about the possibility of being a contributor to your company. Based on our conversation and my understanding of your objectives, I have outlined the specific ways I can be of value on the following pages.

I will call you next week to talk further.

Thank you.

Sincerely,

Brad Osherwitz

Situation E: You discovered a way to create a position for yourself.

Sample Letter E

February 8, 1999

Ms. Flannery Flam
Senior Vice President
The Flamingo Company
6787 Unesco Drive
Austin, TX 78766

Dear Ms. Flam:

Thank you for meeting with me when I was in Austin last week. You were very kind to extend our meeting into lunch. Thank you, too, for a delicious lunch.

I am very impressed with the Flamingo Company and am extremely interested in exploring further how I can contribute my expertise.

As we discussed, I have worked in a similar start-up where I created and implemented a long-range marketing plan that led to the company's record sales and earnings within one year. I also have a successful track record in recruiting and training a professional sales team. These experiences seem to be a perfect match to help your company meet its five-year goals.

I am committed to moving to Austin by the end of this year. To facilitate our exploration of a working relationship, I have enclosed a proposal that outlines your objectives and how I can help you meet them.

I will call you next week to talk further. Thank you again.

Sincerely,

Brad Osherwitz

Situation F: You met someone purely for an informational meeting and want to keep in contact.

Sample Letter F

February 8, 1999

Ms. Lynn Lingo
Greenbriar Chest
8888 North Lamar
Austin, TX 78713

Dear Ms. Lingo:

I appreciate the time you spent with me last week when I was in Austin. Marianne was right when she said you were very knowledgeable about the nonprofit organizations in this area. You not only pointed me in the right direction, but referred me to two terrific marketing professionals.

As it turned out, I did end up meeting with Travis Nowl and Christina Gerrod and plan to follow up on their suggestions when I return to the Austin area in March. I'll let you know how that goes.

In the meantime, I hope you're enjoying your vacation. Thank you again.

Sincerely,

Brad Osherwitz

7

THEY WANT YOU

Isn't it nice to be wanted? That's exactly what it means when a company extends you an offer of employment. They're saying: We like you, we like what you've done in the past (or can see your potential) and think you can help make this a better place now and in the future. In fact, we think you're the best one out there for the job. We will trust you with our trade secrets, special formulas, and all that kind of stuff.

Now is the time to take advantage of this blooming love affair—when they want you and will do anything (within reason) to get you. So assuming you've got an offer on the table or will get one eventually, let's talk about how to build on your position of strength.

DO YOU WANT THE JOB?

First, you need to decide if you like the position and the company and what goes along with that—if it's what you said you wanted in Chapter 1. Remember, you described your next career position in terms of the skills you'll use, the way it will challenge you, the pay you'll receive, and the environment and management you'd like. Let's look at those points in greater detail.

WHAT TO EVALUATE

◆ THE POSITION ITSELF

Based on what you know about the job, will you use your skills? Will you be excited about the projects you'll work on? Will you feel energized and motivated? Will you gain satisfaction from the work? Will you be able to learn new technology or enhance your skills in this position? Is there a more responsible position to aspire to within the company down the road? If you don't know enough about the position to answer these questions, you need to go back to someone at the company and get more information.

◆ THE COMPANY

Can you get excited about what they make or do? Is the company staying abreast of technology? Do they have state-of-the-art equipment? Do you like the direction in which the company is headed? Are they poised for the future? Are they financially viable? Do they have a good reputation? What does the company stand for—does it have a mission statement? If so, do you agree with it?

◆ THE ENVIRONMENT, CULTURE, AND HOW THEY TREAT PEOPLE

Does the environment make employees feel valued? Does the company support the development of its employees and their skills? Do they really mean it if they say they are customer-focused with appropriate infrastructure and investment? Are they as concerned with quality as they are with productivity?

What are the opportunities for women to advance? Are there child-care benefits, flexible hours, and other family-friendly perks?

Is there trust between management and employees? Do employees talk about having fun at work? Do employees get regular performance reviews? On what criteria is performance based? How do people get to key roles in the organization? Is coaching and/or mentoring encouraged? How are new employees assimilated in the company? Is there honest communication about mutual objectives? Does management consider employees' interests in decisions that affect them?

How is individual contribution recognized? Is team effort and success rewarded? How? Are risk-taking and creativity encouraged? How are they rewarded?

◆ THE LEADERSHIP

The environment, culture, and overall success of the company is a result of the people who lead an organization. Even though leadership styles vary, there are some basics that seem to fit the best leaders. According to a *Fortune* magazine article (March 1998) on America's most admired companies, there are five things that leaders must do: (1) establish a sensible direction, (2) inspire people in a way that makes them want to contribute the maximum, (3) create conditions that energize and inspire people, (4) have a knack for allocating capital, (5) be passionate, committed, and love their business. How do the leaders of the company line up?

◆ THE PEOPLE

Who will you report to? Do you feel good about working for that person? Are you clear about reporting relationships? If you will manage people, how do you feel about that team of people?

◆ SALARY AND BENEFITS

How does the company pay compared with its competition? Will you be compensated fairly for the problems you'll face, the responsibility you'll have, the decisions you'll be accountable for to meet the expectations that are required to do a good job? What's your salary potential?

Do the people who have earned it get bonuses and, if applicable, stock ownership? If you get a salary, do you understand what factors it's based on? What's the overall benefits package like?

Not everything about the offer or the company will be perfect. And not all of these issues will be as important to you as they might be to someone else. So rate the position according to what you care about. At the same time, don't slough over these categories, thinking they really don't matter—that you can work anywhere as long as you're making good money.

A television producer who moved from Indiana to New York for his dream job found his life had turned into a nightmare. Once he got into the position he found that he disagreed with management decisions and how they viewed quality. "I was constantly asking myself why we gave up our life for this," he said. Then Ted Turner bought the company and closed it. "My wife was furious that our lives had been turned upside down and her career stalled for a job that went away after sixteen months."

Of course, no one can predict a company's future or how things will turn out, but you owe it to yourself and the people this move affects to ask lots of questions and thoroughly evaluate the situation. You have to like what you're doing, be challenged, feel valued, and believe in the company, *plus* be fairly compensated. Even with a great salary, after the honeymoon is over these other factors *will* matter.

BEFORE YOU ACCEPT

Let's assume you like the position and overall, everything is what you want. Do you just say, "I'll take it"? Nope. First, there are three key things to consider.

◆ 1. WHAT'S NEGOTIABLE

Now—before you respond to the offer—is the time to discuss what you need to have to feel good about accepting the position and moving. If you don't think about this and bring it up now, it's much tougher to get once you've accepted the offer.

Don't worry that the company will think you're being pushy or will get mad and withdraw the offer. If you do this right, you're just being smart. I've never heard of a company withdrawing an offer just because someone countered it. They want you, remember? They'll either try to make you happy or tell you this is as good as it gets.

Benefits and Perks

Just about anything is negotiable. Parking, child care, vacation, company car, continuing education, signing bonuses, performance reviews, flex time, stock options, an office with a view, memberships, relocation expenses. What do you want? Write it all down then prioritize what's most important to you.

Let's assume that relocation expenses and things associated with your move are on your top ten list. Here are the types of things you might ask for:

- Shipment and/or storage of household goods
- Temporary living at your new location
- Expenses incurred during home-hunting trips
- Spouse or partner reemployment assistance
- Day-care–finding assistance

- School selection assistance
- Moving one or two automobiles
- Costs to sell former house, such as real estate agent's commission, attorney fees, tax on transfer of property
- Costs to purchase new home, such as appraisal fees, tax on transfer of real estate, inspections, attorney fees
- Return trips to former location
- Property management or rental of former home
- Child and elder care
- Lease-breaking costs
- Apartment search fees

With so many two-income households, it's not unheard of to ask for lost-wage compensation and career consultation for spouses who quit their jobs to move, says relocation experts Runzheimer International. And as the workplace demographic shifts, it's not unusual for working mothers to ask for day-care–finding assistance or school selection assistance for older children. More single parents means requests for legal assistance to change child custody arrangements.

If you're the primary caregiver of an elderly parent, you might ask for assistance to move your parents or caregiver/facility-finding assistance. Many companies are reviewing their relocation policies to accommodate a work force that is increasingly comprised of females.

Companies also realize that this kind of assistance increases peace of mind and helps people in the move process—which can cut downtime due to personal or family-related problems.

Then there's the "Miscellaneous Allowance." This is a chunk of money that companies base on your salary or pay as a flat amount. This covers things like house hunting, temporary living and en route expenses. Some companies use this to pay for utility and cable TV hookups, driver's license and auto registration, and other incidentals. Since itemizing and documenting expenses is an administrative headache, companies tend to give a lump-sum payment that averages $3,000, say Runzheimer experts.

I've also seen employment offers which gave an employee an additional month's salary to defray moving costs. By the way, most relocation-expense reimbursements and payments are considered income and are subject to tax.

If you are a recent college graduate, relocation benefits don't look as promising. Most companies won't offer much to recent college graduates, according to the folks at Runzheimer.

But don't shy away from negotiating for the best offer for an entry level position. Also, signing bonuses are not uncommon—especially in technical industries.

Benefits also depend on whether you're working for a small, medium, or large company or for the government.

Salary

Of course, salary is also negotiable, so fine-tune your negotiating skills. Keep in mind that incomes will vary according to the geographic area. According to a study conducted by management consultants Abbott, Langer & Associates, there are disparities in white-collar, technical, and blue-collar jobs.

For instance, receptionists in the New York and New Jersey metropolitan area do 29 percent better than the national average, and in Butler County, Missouri, they are 39 percent below the national average. Drafters are paid 38 percent above the national average in the New York City metropolitan area and 22 percent below the average in Lexington, Kentucky. Maintenance machinists are paid best in San Jose, California; forklift operators are paid 47 percent above average in Ann Arbor, Michigan, and the least in the Rio Grande Valley, Texas, area at 52 percent below the national average.

In Alaska, computer operators are paid 60 percent more and

word-processing operators are paid 24 percent more than the national average. But the cost of living in Alaska is also significantly higher than anywhere else in the U.S., says the report.

Another study conducted by consultants William M. Mercer, Inc., confirms that salaries paid for equivalent jobs in the same company can also vary dramatically depending on the geographic area. For example, a middle management or technical position might pay $50,000 in Milwaukee or Minneapolis. The same job in San Jose, California, will pay $59,700.

If you have questions about salary or benefits packages, write, call or e-mail the folks at the Employee Benefits Research Institute at 2121 K Street, NW, Suite 600, Washington, DC 20037; (202) 659-0670; http://www.ebri.org.

Check the International Salary Calculator web site at http://www2.homefair.com/calc/sa/ca/c.html. Make sure you also check the cost-of-living information I list in the Appendix, so you are working with realistic data.

◆ 2. WHAT IF THE JOB DOESN'T WORK OUT

A woman once wrote me that she was nearing negotiations for a position that would involve a geographical move. Besides the company paying for moving expenses, temporary housing, and helping her husband find a new job, she was wondering if there was anything else she should ask for. I suggested she ask for a severance package in the event that something changes and the job doesn't work out for whatever reason once she packed up and moved. Why not? Otherwise, you're the one taking on most of the risk.

A severance package is a benefit that's becoming more accepted as companies go through change. It might include:

- Severance pay (can range from two weeks to six months' pay)

- Payment of health insurance premiums (can range from ninety days to a year)
- Payment of bonus, incentive, or profit-sharing compensation had employment continued throughout the year
- Release from noncompete contract
- Payment of outplacement service
- Continuation of voice mail privileges until reemployed
- Paying for your moving expenses
- Paying for unused vacation time
- Agreeing not to contest your right to unemployment compensation
- A favorable letter of reference
- Use of your office until you get a new job
- Payment for continued education

Packages are based on your level and the length of time you've been with a company, with a six-month severance arrangement the most common for someone earning more than $80,000. Without being greedy, think about what you will need in the event that things don't work out. You may not get everything you want, but it can't hurt to ask.

◆ 3. NONCOMPETE CONTRACTS

Don't be surprised if an employer asks you to sign something that says you can't work in your industry for up to two years if you leave, get laid off, or fired. More people—and it's not just senior executives—are being handed noncompete contracts that can restrict their future freedom to work.

Since it's getting tougher and tougher for companies to find good people, there's been an increase in "restrictive covenants" (the generic term describing promises made by employees to their employers).

Contracts like noncompete agreements help employers protect

their investment in people and reduce executive search costs and training. They also "thwart the possibility of losing precious trade secrets and business plans" to competitors, according to New York attorney Alan Sklover, who specializes in executive employment issues.

The standard noncompete agreement goes something like this: "For six months after I leave my employment here I will not work in Michigan, Chicago, or Atlanta for a firm which directly competes with my employer."

Time restrictions in working for a competitor can be from six months to two years. The time and territory covered will depend on the nature of your business. And generally a noncompete is effective whether your job has been eliminated, you've been fired, or you leave voluntarily, says Sklover.

An agreement could state: "If I receive an offer of outside employment, before I accept that offer of employment, I must give notice to my employer, and provide my employer with an opportunity to match that offer. If my employer matches that offer, I will remain."

Another kind of restrictive covenant says, "If I voluntarily leave employment with the Company within two years, I will not take employment elsewhere until I have repaid to the Company its expenses incurred in my relocation and recruitment." (If you do sign such an agreement, make sure you know the exact figure of this commitment.)

These restrictive covenants or clauses in an employment contract usually come with an inducement: perks such as a generous sign-on bonus, an expensive relocation package, even an employment guarantee. What should you do if you're asked to sign one?

- Read it carefully. Review it with an attorney.
- Like any contract, you don't have to accept all the terms. Sklover suggests you ask (1) that the noncompete apply only

if you leave your job voluntarily (why should you agree not to work for anyone else if you're laid off or are fired?) and (2) for a more limited definition of "the competition."

- Don't be afraid to ask that restrictions be removed since it's a risk of forced unemployment or forced employment outside your field or geographic area.
- Take noncompetes seriously. When you're being lured with perks, you might be tempted to sign almost anything—especially if you're convinced a court won't enforce it, he says. "Restrictive covenants are a potent weapon in the competition for unique business talent and should not be underestimated."

Most courts will enforce reasonable noncompetes. In some cases, courts have been reluctant to tell anyone they can't make a living. Other times, courts will say to an employee, " 'If you agreed to it, and took a job on that basis, perhaps even accepted a sign-on bonus and relocation monies, you must live with it,' " says Sklover.

This whole noncompete thing makes me squirm. I'd think long and hard before signing a restrictive covenant that could deny you the opportunity to make a living in your chosen field—especially when you're moving to take a new job.

HOW TO ASK FOR WHAT YOU WANT

Earlier I said that if you counter an offer in the right way, you don't need to be concerned about seeming pushy or that the company will get mad and withdraw the offer. The right way means that you:

- Don't ask for anything—salary, benefits or anything else—*before* you've received the offer. I don't care if you think you're on the verge of getting an offer; the company hinted they're interested in hiring you; they've said they're getting close to making an offer; or if you think you've hit it off so well they can't possibly *not* offer you the job. If you have not actually heard or seen on paper the words, "We would like to offer you the position of (whatever)"—or words to that effect—you don't have an offer.

If the hiring manager asks you what salary you want, that is not an offer. By the way, if you are asked about salary before you're made an offer, it's perfectly fine to respond with something like:

"At this point I'd like to concentrate on the position and to explore if it's a good fit. Once we've both decided I'm right for the position, then it would make sense to discuss compensation." That's not being pushy either.

If there is a question in your mind as to whether you're being offered a position at any point in the interview process, simply ask, "Are you offering me the position?"

If you do discuss any of these issues before you get an offer, you lose your negotiating power because they haven't said they want you yet. Many times interviewers are looking for a reason to rule you out of the running. If you mention salary that's too high—or low—you could have just given them that.

• First tell of your interest in the position, then start negotiating. Once the company has made an offer, tell them how interested and enthusiastic you are about the potential match. You might even touch upon some aspect of the job to which you feel you bring particular value. This is the time to negotiate salary and benefits. Don't just accept the first offer. The first offer is usually just that—a first offer. If your experience and the responsibilities of the job warrant a higher salary, speak up. Then, open up the discussion on other issues that are important to you. Say something like:

"Before I make a decision, there are a few things I'd like to talk about. How does the Mars and Venus Company handle a trailing spouse? . . . Since my husband will have to leave his job, what type of assistance do you offer? . . . Could you tell me about your relocation package?"

GET IT IN WRITING

Get the offer in writing so that you're clear on exactly what it entails. (See the sample letters at the end of this chapter.) If the company hasn't said when they want your reply, ask. Do not give your response at the time of the offer. You need time to mull it over in your own head and talk to your spouse or a close friend. Sleep on it. Take at least a day or two. You may even be looking at two offers at the same time and need to buy some time, which I'll talk about next.

IF YOU GET MORE THAN ONE OFFER

One of my clients had been job hunting for six months. He had a nibble or two, but nothing he was jumping for joy over. All of a sudden, things started to gel. He got an offer he liked from a large company, but wasn't thrilled about the pay or the location, which was in a small town in Illinois. The company insisted on having his answer within a few days.

The week prior he had an interview at a smaller firm in Virginia. He liked the job, the potential for international experience, the pay, and the location. The company was still interviewing candidates, so no decision had been made. The owner had to go out of the country and wouldn't be back for another week, which further delayed the interview process. Meanwhile, the first company wouldn't budge on its time frame. Even though he told them he needed more time and that he felt rushed about making the decision, they wouldn't give him any longer to make his decision.

"What should I do?" he called me up and asked. "I like the Virginia company, but who knows when they'll make a decision?

I'm satisfied with the other offer, but would like to be able to compare the two before I make a decision."

We discussed the pros and cons of the two positions and how he would feel if he declined the larger company's offer. He didn't want to lose that opportunity, but he also didn't want to have to withdraw his acceptance if he got a better offer later. At the same time, he felt the company wasn't giving him much of a choice due to the pressure to respond. So he accepted the first company's offer, knowing that he might turn around and withdraw it later—and not feeling good about potentially doing that.

At the same time, he contacted the other company, told them about the offer, and asked if they could speed up their decision-making. The president, who was back in town, asked him to fly back to Virginia the next day. He did, was offered the position and, a day later, accepted. Now he had to send a letter back to the first company declining the offer he had already accepted.

For whatever reason, the Illinois company didn't give him the time he needed. It's really smart on the company's part to give you as much time as you need (within reason) to respond to an offer. A former human resources professional at Procter & Gamble told me, "We wanted our candidates to be sure they were accepting our position with their full commitment. We knew that if we forced a decision deadline, we could be stiffed. We also knew that a candidate who was not fully committed to P&G would always be wondering, 'What if . . .' and would have one eye on the door."

If you are in a situation where you feel you need to renege on an offer, be gracious, apologetic for any inconvenience, and appreciative of the offer.

EVERYTHING AT ONCE

This whole process is very unpredictable, but one thing seems to be consistent. If you've been diligent in your follow-up, stayed focused and committed to your strategy—even during the down times—everything seems to pop at the same time. You've planted enough seeds and they've had time to germinate. Then all of a sudden offers happen. People you've been corresponding with for months call about an opening.

So now you've got a new set of issues to deal with: Should I take one of these or keep looking? Be as objective as you can in evaluating your job search efforts. Have you done enough to dig up the best offer? Have you really evaluated each offer thoroughly?

THREE MORE THINGS TO DO

Now that you've accepted an offer, you've got three new areas to contend with: (1) giving notice at your present job, if you're working, (2) letting people know about your new position, and (3) planning your move.

◆ 1. GIVE NOTICE

Graceful is the key word here. Even if you hate the company, your boss, and everything about the place and have been counting the seconds until you could walk out the door knowing you're never coming back, do not burn your bridges. Write a brief letter of resignation and hand-deliver it at the time you plan to tell your boss you're leaving. In this letter share your appreciation for the opportunity to work at the company, your last day of work, and, if you want, what your next move is. In your conversation, say the same kinds of things.

Go through the projects you're working on and determine the best way to hand them off if they won't be completed before you leave. Offer to meet with and even train the person who will take over your responsibilities.

When do you tell your company you're leaving? That depends

on your industry and your company. Some places may want you out of there the minute you tell them you're resigning. It also depends on the starting date at your new job. Give at least two weeks' notice.

And while you're still there, don't turn each day into a gripe session about the company or the job. Just as you went into your job search looking for what you wanted to move towards (not what you wanted to get away from), let people know what your objective has been. If you have an exit interview, offer constructive feedback.

Here's a possibility that you might want to prepare for. What if, when you give your notice, your company makes a counteroffer? They offer you an even higher salary and the office with the closed door you've been groveling for—if you'll please stay. Here is someone else saying, "We want you . . . and we don't want you to leave." Tempting to take? Go back and look at your "What's Important to Me" Worksheet and *your* Reason for Moving Statement. Remind yourself why you were looking for greener pastures in the first place. This is the moment of truth.

◆ 2. UPDATE YOUR CHEERLEADERS

Think of all the people who have been involved in this process with you: Your first group of contacts on your lists of People in the City Where I Live and People I Already Know in My Target Area, folks you met on the fly, recruiters, people you interviewed with, people you met online in chat rooms and newsgroups, colleagues from professional meetings and job focus groups, business executives you read about and talked to and got referred to by others. They all played a part. One thing led to another. They all invested their time to help you. They deserve to know how things ended up.

You'll want to call some people and write to others. If you kept your Move Manifesto updated as you met people, you can do this easily by going through your lists. If there are a lot of people on your lists, develop a generic letter to let them know the place you're moving, the company, your position, how you can be reached, and how much you appreciate their help. Even if you didn't find the person very helpful, send the letter. There's a sample at the end of this chapter.

You not only owe this much to the people who helped you, you owe it to yourself. This is how you build those sincere relationships we talked about way back in Chapter 2. You started off by asking for their help, now you're letting them know where you'll be so you can both keep in contact and you can help *them* in the future. If you don't do things like this, you're guilty of going on the hunt for people who can be useful to your career when you need them. That's how networking got a bad rap.

◆ 3. PLAN YOUR MOVE

What's a Write-off?

Add a new section to your Move Manifesto that holds receipts for your expenses and any other documents pertaining to your job search and move. Get the Internal Revenue Service's forms for Job Search Expenses (Publications #17 and #529) and Moving Expenses (Publication #521) to know what you can and cannot deduct. Other IRS publications also mention specifics such as interview expenses (publication #535) and transportation expenses (#463). Another thing you can do is get a copy of the Guide to Free Tax Services (#910), which describes the IRS publications and subject matter in them. The number to call at the IRS is (800) 829-3676.

Based on the IRS 1997 rules, the following job search expenses are tax deductible if you're searching in the same occupation you have now, even if you don't get the job:

- Employment and outplacement agency fees
- Résumé preparation (typing, printing, mailing)
- Travel and transportation expenses for a trip that is primarily to look for a new job. If the trip is not primarily to look for a new job but you have expenses on the trip while looking for a new job, you can deduct those expenses even if you don't deduct the travel expenses.

You cannot deduct expenses if you are searching for a job in a different occupation or if you are seeking employment for the first time.

Based on the IRS 1997 rules, moving household goods, travel, and lodging are tax deductible if:

- Your expenses are incurred within one year from your start of work at your new location. (Expenses can be deducted if circumstances prevented your move within the first year.) You don't have to arrange to work before you move to a new locale. But you do need to actually go to work.
- Your move meets the distance test established by the IRS. That is, that your new job is at least fifty miles farther from your former home than your old main job location. For example, if your old job was ten miles from your former home, your new job must be at least sixty miles from that former home.
- Your move meets the time test. This means you must work full-time for at least 39 weeks the first year of your move. If you're self-employed, you must work full-time for 78 weeks during the first two years as self-employed and/or as an employee.

Minor Details

Decide what to keep, give away, donate, or sell at a yard sale. If you're paying for your move, reserve a rental truck or select a moving company and get insurance coverage. You can get estimates from more than three hundred moving companies at www.movequotes.com.

One of my clients who was paying for her own move needed to keep her costs low. So she and her husband rented a truck for their belongings, paid her father-in-law and his friend to drive the truck from Ohio to Arizona, and bought them return-trip plane tickets. She drove their five cats out in her car and a few days later her husband came with the three dogs in a rental car. The total cost was about $2,000.

Around a month before you move, complete a Change of Address form that you get at your local post office. If you're moving to a temporary living space, make arrangements to put things in storage. One woman moved in for six months with a roommate she found by answering an ad in a religious newspaper. She put most of her belongings in storage, which cost her around $60 a month. Yes, she had to pay moving costs again when she moved permanently.

Some people choose to move into temporary living spaces so they can get to the know the area better before locking themselves into a lease or purchase. Often, there's just not enough time to find permanent housing.

A couple weeks before moving day, call your phone, cable, heat and electric and water companies to stop your utilities at your old address and start service at your new address.

ON MOVING DAY

Be there when the movers arrive. They may have questions. Plus, you want to keep an eye on their activities. Walk through every room with them as they create an inventory of your belongings. Double-check their descriptions of what they record in the inventory. Don't leave until the last item is loaded on the truck.

Make sure the driver has your correct new address, clear directions on how to get there, and a phone number where you can be reached. Get his or her name.

BY THE WAY . . . CONGRATULATIONS

Now let's talk about how to keep all your hard work working for you as you put down roots and build a new life.

Sample Job Offer Letter

Figs & Dates, Incorporated
102 Dried Fruit Way
Columbia, SC 29215

June 5, 1999

Ms. Penelope Pistachio
2020 Largo Road
Ludlow, VT 05149

Dear Ms. Pistachio:

I am pleased to extend an offer of employment with Figs & Dates, Incorporated, for the position of the Director of Quality Control. This position is located in Columbia, South Carolina. Your gross annual salary would be $70,000 and is paid biweekly. In addition, under the bonus plan, you can earn up to $10,000 based on your division's performance and up to 100 percent of this figure based on your performance. This would be prorated during your first year, based on our fiscal year.

As an employee, you will also be eligible to participate in Figs & Dates Comprehensive Benefits Plan. Figs & Dates will cover all normal moving costs as outlined in the enclosed Relocation Brochure. Your relocations package includes a lump-sum payment of $5,000 to be used to cover apartment hunting, temporary living, and en route expenses.

We are excited about the prospect of you joining our team and believe your skills and background will add much value to our company, while the position will give you the type of challenge and career growth you are seeking. We would appreciate receiving written confirmation of your decision by June 15, 1999. Please send your signed confirmation to Sylvia Stem-Pitt at the address on this letterhead. Please call me if you have any questions.

Sincerely,

Richard Seed

Sample Job Offer Letter

Venus Medical Hospital
200 East Wisconsin Avenue
Milwaukee, WI 53201
(414) 291-0000

May 22, 1999

Mr. Luis Frimkin
5678 Jefferson
St. Louis, MO 63103

Dear Luis:

We are pleased to confirm our offer of employment to you. Your title will be Certified Phlebotomist. Your compensation will be $2,800 per month, to be paid twice per month. You will receive a signing bonus of $4,000 less taxes. You will receive this check within two weeks of your hire date.

The Venus Medical Hospital offers a variety of benefits for you and your family including:

• Eleven holidays per year, vacation, short- and long-term disability or pay continuation, medical leave, military leave and family leave of absence.

• A comprehensive health care plan, dental option, vision plan, long-term disability package; life insurance program, Employee Assistance Program, maternity planning, child care and elder care.

To assist you with your relocation from St. Louis to Milwaukee, we offer you relocation benefits that you will find outlined in the enclosed Venus Relocation Program. You will receive up to five nights and six days for house hunting and thirty days' temporary living allowance.

This offer is contingent upon your successful completion of a medical evaluation, including testing for the presence of drugs. You must also meet the requirements of a security background check and provide proof of your eligibility to work in the United States.

This offer is further contingent upon your agreement that if you voluntarily terminate your employment with Venus Medical Center within one year of the effective date of your employment, you will reimburse Venus Medical Center for all relocation expenses.

This offer will remain open until June 11, 1999. Please sign this letter and return it to me with your start date indicated as a formal acceptance of this offer. Please call me at (414) 291-0000 with any questions.

Sincerely,

Milligan Tinster
Human Resources Director

_____   _____

Accepted   Date

_____

Start Date

Sample New Job Announcement Letter

Laird Hazenowski
421 Perpetual Way
Leonia, NJ 07606

July 8, 1999

Mr. Luciano Sigliani
69 East 10th Street
New York, NY 10003

Dear Lu:

I'm writing to share the good news about my recent career move. You were instrumental in helping me discover this new position, so I not only want to thank you but tell you a little about where I'll be moving.

After four months of research and interviews with companies in the Minneapolis area, I met with the president of a small start-up firm that makes outerwear and skiwear and is quickly making a name for itself in this market. Over the last three years the company has experienced a 30 percent growth.

Timing is everything, for the president was looking for someone with my exact experience to help her move into the Asian and European markets. I will start in my new position as Director of International Sales at the end of this month.

I can't thank you enough for your wise counsel, our Saturday morning chats, and the referrals to Genevieve Gumectihide and Angela Foe. Please keep in contact and let me know how your trips to Europe go this fall. If you're ever in the Minneapolis area, I hope you'll let me know. My new address is 609 Hellbent Lane, Minneapolis, MN 55401. I'll contact you when I know my new phone number.

Thank you again.

Sincerely,

Laird Hazenowski

8

FINDING YOUR WAY
AT WORK AND HOME

Now that you're all moved in, you may be wondering, as you sit surrounded by boxes packed with all your stuff in a new house or apartment on a street and in a place where you don't know a soul, "Now why did I do this?"

This is another one of those times when your Move Manifesto comes in handy. Turn to the page with *Your* Reason for Moving Statement. It should lighten your load and renew your high hopes for a fresh beginning.

No matter how much you wanted this, planned the steps, and waited for this day, expect stress. On the homefront, you may be living in temporary quarters for a while with most of your worldly goods in storage.

You might still be dealing with the effects of the move. I don't know too many people who have moved—even across town—who don't have a moving nightmare story to tell.

Even if you moved with a partner, it can get lonely. You'll miss your friends and family—anything familiar.

A single man who moved from Oklahoma to Ohio told me, "I knew no one, left all my friends behind, and literally started my life over. The first two years were very depressing socially."

It doesn't have to be that way. Remember the man I mentioned in Chapter 5 who attended a Big Brother/Big Sister benefit party when he was checking out the city? He ended up moving to this city, and as a result of his earlier efforts, had several new friends the day he moved to town. He also joined a synagogue and its young adult congregation, attended its adult Sunday school classes, and got involved in a fund-raising campaign. Within the first few months of living in his new home, he had developed dozens of new friends and colleagues and had an active social life.

"It's tough not to fall back into patterns of the last place where you lived . . . wanting to have the same types of activities and friends. You have to reach out and be open," he explains.

TIPS FOR THE NEW KID ON THE BLOCK

• Give yourself time to acclimate to your new hometown.

If you can, don't start working right away. Unpack, stroll, drive around, and get comfortable. Find new doctors, a good dry cleaner, a suitable bank, get your cable installed, blinds up— whatever you need to feel at home.

One of my clients was overwhelmed with of all the "little things that take an inordinate amount of time and energy that we didn't think of. Things like getting a new driver's license, car registration, settling with the sellers of the house we bought who didn't fix what they were supposed to fix.

"The electric utility company requires credit references or a large security deposit and you have to fill out a two-page application. Car insurance was difficult to get. Things that were a phone call away back home are a real pain here."

You've probably been working with someone at your new company by telephone to help coordinate the details of your move and new employment. This person might also be a good resource to help you with those things.

• Be prepared to tire easily.

Once you do start your new job, you'll be learning new things, meeting new people, and getting to know their styles. You'll feel pressure to look good, get up to speed, contribute, and show your worth. All of that is tiring.

• Take it slow.

Do a lot of listening the first few weeks at work. Ask questions. Go to lunch with people. Don't make big, impactful decisions at first.

• Create reasonable expectations.

When you start something new—especially a new job—you'll feel overwhelmed with all the information you don't know and new internal processes, and procedures. Give yourself a break. Don't expect to understand everything right away. Acclimating on the job is a process too.

• Continue building your network.

Now that you're here you can have more frequent contact with the people you met when you were conducting your long-distance campaign. Go to lunch with your new associates. Pick up the phone and check in every once in a while.

• Don't forget people from your past.

Keep your old friends and associates updated through e-mail and occasional phone calls. When you move away and get caught up in your new life, it's easy to forget who helped you get there. That's another way networking got a bad reputation.

• Expose yourself to new situations.

Once you're more settled, put yourself in new situations outside the workplace. This will not only help you socially but professionally too. Volunteering is a great way for you and a trailing partner to meet new people. And if your partner hasn't yet found a new position, it's also a way to test the waters of a new profession, develop new skills, beef up experience, and make new friends.

There are plenty of places that could use you. I looked up "United Way" on the Internet and found United Way offices all over the country offering volunteer opportunities. I did a more general search for "Volunteer Opportunities" and found 177 matches. There were listings in specific locales such as Chicago, San Francisco, Philadelphia, Minnesota, and others. And specific listings for just about anybody you can think of—Quakers, various religions, kids, child advocacy organizations, the Oregon Caves National Monument . . . you name it.

Think about issues that matter to you. What problems in society do you want to help solve? Some communities have volunteer clearinghouses. You tell them what you're interested in and they refer you to agencies that match your interests.

• Look for visible projects to work on in a nonprofit agency, human services, an arts or civic organization, or a city-sponsored event.

This will help you become more visible in the community. Check out community agencies who need people to serve on committees and their board of directors.

OTHER ISSUES THAT CROP UP

◆ AN UNEMPLOYED PARTNER

One couple I know decided to move separately. "Our intention was to do a two-city marriage for the first six months because my wife didn't want to leave her employer yet. But after a month of separation punctuated by 'conjugal visits' alternating between Stamford and Indianapolis, she decided it was better to pull the plug and head east."

Now they had to deal with her need to find a job. "I was unemployed for three months—which were hell," she describes. "I had never been unemployed and fell into all the traps: staying up to all hours, sleeping until noon, not dressing until my husband came home, watching too much TV. Because I was home, I felt obligated to clean and cook, which I hate to do. Then I took a $10,000 pay cut to enter a computer systems analysis trainee program. Things were better when I became employed, but at thirty, I was the den mother of four young male trainees who had never worked before. The job was not very fulfilling and I very much resented our move."

Being unemployed and underemployed can be a real issue for your partner. Look at the options available. One might be part-time work that could lead to a full-time job. Many people—lawyers, accountants, clerical and blue-collar workers—have joined the part-time workforce. And many companies do offer benefits to part-timers. Some firms offer benefits on a prorated basis depending on the number of hours you work or how long you've been at the company. For instance, if you work three days a week, you may get 75 percent of the vacation time a full-time employee gets.

I talked about temporary work in Chapter 5, which is also a good way for a trailing partner to try out various companies while adjusting to a new home.

Help him or her build new alliances through the people you now know. A 1997 *New York Times* article talked about how successful women build alliances rather than networks. They rely on strategic alliances, the kind formed by working on tasks or serving on boards. This "alliancing" takes advantage of the natural relationships that grow between colleagues, says the article. And these relationships ended up playing a major role in the progress of their careers.

Encourage your partner to join a professional association, a job search focus group—all the things you did way back in earlier chapters to get your job search in gear. The principles are the same.

♦ A COMMUTING PARTNER

One of you may stay behind to handle the sale of your home or take care of the kids, who are finishing out a school year. Commuting back and forth on weekends, or not seeing each other for months, can be stressful. Talk on the phone frequently, write or use e-mail to keep in touch. And, remember, this is a temporary inconvenience.

◆ KIDS' SPECIAL NEEDS

If you have children, it's important for them to meet local children in the first few days of your move. These first contacts may not turn out to be their best friends, but it will start the process. Neighbor children and coworkers' kids are a good place to begin.

Let them keep in contact with special friends back home. If the distance isn't too far, you might even have friends from the old neighborhood visit. Allow them to call friends from back home periodically. Encourage them to write or e-mail friends.

At the same time, make sure they're not living in the past. One woman told me about her fourteen-year-old niece who didn't want to move and leave her friends when her family moved to a new city. When she and her family did move she joined the cross-country and track teams, found part-time work at a kennel, and found a youth church group, but she kept in daily contact with her old friends via e-mail. She knew everything that happened there. She talked about her old friends incessantly to her new acquaintances and one day several of them said, "Stop living in the past. Let it go!" In this case, e-mail became a crutch and didn't help her adjust to her new home.

The Employment Relocation Council even suggests providing your children with pen pals from company families or schools in the new location in the months prior to the move. This way they can learn about the new location through the eyes of someone their age and it gives them a chance to make a new friend before they move.

Find scouting groups or activities they had enjoyed at their former home. Hold weekly family meetings to see how things are going. Have dinner together. Plan how you'll decorate the house. Make volunteering a family project.

FINDING HAPPINESS IN YOUR GREENER PASTURE

It will take time. But before you know it, the last box will be unpacked and sitting by the curb for the trash collectors. You'll have shortcuts to your new office down pat. You'll be accepting invitations to barbecues. You'll even find time to reflect on how far you've come since you first sat down and figured out why you wanted to move to greener pastures.

My hope is that you will be as content as the client I told you about in Chapter 5—the one whose husband had been saying since they married, "Within five years, we'll be living in Arizona," and five years came and went and finally they moved and started fresh. When I told her I was writing this book and asked her how things were going, she wrote me to say:

"Each night we're out in our backyard with our three dogs, the Verde Valley stretching before us, the mountains off to the west. Clarice might chase a jackrabbit, Fred has his nose to the ground, and little Harold is trotting along the trail. There might be an incredible sunset, the earthy fragrance of the creosote bush, a breeze cooling us for a moment, or one of a dozen things that makes us sigh and realize that we are where we belong."

Happy trails to you, too.

Appendix

HELPFUL RESOURCES

RESEARCH

◆ Information on Locales and Cost of Living
Location Guides: Publishes Top Ten List, The Location Digest,
The Location Report
www.locationguides.com
P.O. Box 58506, Salt Lake City, UT 94158
(801) 645-7252

America's Career InfoNet (through www.ajb.dni.us/)
Click "Geographic Profile" for state's demographics and economic development

Runzheimer International's cost of living index ($25)
Runzheimer International
Runzheimer Park, Rochester, WI 53167
(414) 767-2200
www.runzheimer.com

Money Magazine annual survey of The Best Places to Live
www.pathfinder.com/money/bestplaces/

American Chamber of Commerce Researchers Association
Most public libraries

www.bigbook.com

http://www.piperinfor.com/state/states.html (state and local gov-
ernments)

http://www.city.net/ (has city Yellow Pages and airline fares)

Bureau of Labor Statistics
http://stats.bls.gov/blshome.html

Datamasters
http://www.datamasters.com

Salary Calculator
http://www2.homefair.com/calc/sa/ca/c.html

Employee Benefits Research Institute
2121 K Street, N.W., Suite 600
Washington, DC 20037
(202) 659-0670
http://www.ebri.org

◆ SOURCES FOR INFORMATION ON BUSINESSES

American Business Information Directory
Directory and CD-ROMs at most public libraries
www.salesleadsusa.com
Purchase lists: (888) 725-3753

U.S. Big Business Directory
www.salesleadsusa.com
Purchase lists: (888) 725-3753

American Manufacturers Directory
Most public libraries

Standard & Poor's Register
Most public libraries

LibrarySpot
www.libraryspot.com

Inc. Magazine/Fastest growing private companies in America
http://www.inc.com/500/

http://www.bigbook.com/

Business Newsbank
(800) 762-8182

General Business File
Most public libraries

New York Public Library: How to Find U.S. Company
Information
http://gopher.nypl.org/research/sibl/company/companyinfo.html

Chamber of Commerce
http://www.chamber-of-commerce.com/
http://www.worldchambers.com/chambers/
http://www.worldchambers.com/registry/ussearch.htm

Public Register's Annual Report Service (order annual reports—
free of charge, view corporate financial profile, financial press
releases and more; has direct links to company's Homepage)
http://www.prars.com/

Bizweb
http://www.bizweb.com/

Smart Business Supersite
http://www.smartbiz.com

Hoovers Online
http://www.hoovers.com

Jobtrack
www.jobtrak.com/profiles

Dow Jones Interactive Publishing
http://ip.dowjones.com

Thomas Register
www.thomasregister.com

Site Net Magazine
www.siteselection.com/

Vault Reports
http://www.vaultreports.com

America's Career InfoNet (through America's Job Bank)
www.ajb.dni.us/

Business Week's Best Companies for Work and Family
http://www.businessweek.com/index.html (for magazine)

Fortune's "The 100 Best Companies to Work for in America"
http://www.pathfinder.com/fortune/1998/980112/int.html

Fortune for the magazine and such lists as "50 Best Companies for Asians, Blacks and Hispanics," "Cool Companies," "America's Largest Companies"
http://www.fortune.com

Working Mother's "Best Companies for Working Mothers"
http://www.womweb.com/index.html

The Corporate Report Card
(Dutton)

Hoover's Top 2,500 Employers
(Hoover's Business Press)

◆ SOURCES FOR JOB DESCRIPTIONS
The Big Book of Jobs
(VGM)

The O*Net Dictionary of Occupational Titles
(JIST)

Dictionary of Occupational Titles
(VGM)

The American Almanac of Jobs and Salaries
(Avon)

◆ CAREER-RELATED CHAT ROOMS
www.clickit.com/bizwiz/bizwiz.htm

www.aboutwork.com

www.talkcity.com

◆ INFORMATION ON TRADE ORGANIZATIONS
National Trade & Professional Associations of the United States
(Columbia Books)

International Association of Conference Centers
www.iacconline.com/

The Professional Convention Management Association
www.pcma.org/

Encyclopedia of Associations (Gale)
(800) 887-Gale
www.gale.com

JOB OPPORTUNITIES

◆ BOOKS ON CAREER INTERNET INFORMATION:
*CareerXRoads, the 1998 Directory to the 500 Best Job, Résumé and
Career Management Sites on the World Wide Web*
(MMC Group)

The Guide to Internet Job Searching
(VGM)

Finding a Job on the Internet,
Alfred and Emily Glossbrenner
(McGraw Hill)

Electronic Job Search Revolution,
Kennedy & Morrow
(Wiley)

Be Your Own Headhunter Online,
Dixon & Tiersten
(Random House)

◆ **Executive Recruiter Sources**
The Directory of Executive Recruiters (Kennedy Publications)
(can purchase labels: (800) 531-0007)

www.HeadHunter.net

Management Recruiters International
www.mrinet.com

The New Career Makers
John Sibbald
(Harper Business)

Job Seekers Guide to Executive Recruiters
Christopher Hunt and Scott Scanlon
(Wiley)

◆ **Multicultural Intern and Recruitment Program**
American Association of Advertising Agencies
www.commercepark.com/aaaa/

American Association of Medical Colleges, minority recruitment
program
www.aamc.org/meded/minority/recruit/start.htm

◆ **Online Temporary Job Service**
www.interim.com

◆ **Online Sites That Advertise Positions**
NETSHARE (for senior executives; you subscribe)
www.netshare.com

America's Job Bank
http://www.ajb.dni.us/

Classified Warehouse
http://www.classifiedwarehouse.com/index.html

Best Jobs in the USA Today
www.bestjobsusa.com/

CareerMosaic
http://www.careermosaic.com

The Monster Board
www.monster.com/

The *Wall Street Journal* Interactive Edition
http://careers.wsj.com

CareerWeb
http://www.cweb.com/

E-Span
http://www.espan.com

MedSearch America (health care jobs)
http://www.medsearch.com/

Online Career Center (browse jobs by city and state)
http://www.occ.com

Today's Classifieds
http://www.nando.net/classads/

Job Link USA
http://www.joblink-usa.com/

Job Trak
http://www.jobtrak.com

http://www.piperinfo.com/state/states.html (city and state job listings)

◆ Résumé Data Bases
Careerweb.com/register/

http://www.espan.com

http://www.medsearch.com/

http://www.occ.com/

http://careers.news-observer.com/

http://www.joblink-usa.com

TRAVEL

◆ Online Services That Create Maps/Information on Construction Delay
Expedia.com

www.movequest.com

MapQuest
www.mapquest.com

Rand Mcnally
www.randmcnally.com

Mapblast
www.mapblast.com

Interstate 95 Exit Information Guide
www.usaster.com/i95/homepage.htm (has information pertinent to traveling on Interstate 95)

The WWWSpeedtrap Registry (just what it sounds like)
www.speedtrap.com/

◆ Information on Low-Cost Goods and Services
www.econet.org/frugal/visions.html

www.usastar.com/i95/homepage.htm

Hotel Reservation Network
www.180096hotel.com

expedia.com (lowest published airfares)

http://www.bestfares.com/

http://www.air-fare.com/

◆ AIRPLANE PRICING AND TICKETING
The Trip
http://flight.thetrip.com
http://flight.thetrip.com/flightstatus/ (checks status of plane)

http://www.city.net/

◆ HOTELS
http://www.all-hotels.com/

http://www.travelweb.com/

http://www.hotelstravel.com/chains.html

◆ BUSINESS-FRIENDLY AND EXTENDED-STAY HOTELS
Hilton Garden Inns
www.hilton.com/ushotels/garden.html
(800) HILTONS

Sheraton Four Points Hotels
www.fourpoints.com/

Residence Inns
http://www.residenceinn.com

Marriott
www.marriott.com/search/featuresearch.asp (pick hotel features)

◆ HOTEL, MOTEL, AND RESTAURANT RATINGS AND GUIDES
www.mapquest.com (*Mobil Travel Guide*)

http://www.menusonline.com

http://www.l.localeyes.com (plus florists, golf, furniture, lawyers, and more)

◆ AIRPORT RENTAL CAR RATES
BreezeNet Guide to Airport Rental Cars
www.bnm.com/rcar.htm

◆ WEATHER SOURCES
National Weather Service
weather.noaa.gov/weather/

The Weather Channel
www.weather.com

Intellicast
www.intellicast.com

AccuWeather
www.accuweather.com

WeatherPost
www.weatherpost.com

America's Career InfoNet
www.ajb.dni.us/

RELOCATION

◆ INFORMATION ON MOVING COMPANIES
www.movequotes.com

◆ ONLINE SITES WITH INFORMATION ON RELOCATION
America's Career Info Net (through America's Job Bank home-page)
www.ajb.dni.us/

Consider Relocation
www.acinet.org/resource/relocate

◆ ONLINE REAL ESTATE SITES
realtor.com

quicken.com (mortgage information)

coldwellbanker.com

century21.com

cyberhomes.com (multiple listing service)

www.homepath.com (starter kit to purchase)

www.homeshark.com (resource for buyers and sellers)

American Homeowners Association (information on buying and selling)
ahahome.com

National Association of Realtors
www.realtorads.com

◆ SOURCES ON MOVING WITH CHILDREN
Let's Make A Move! A Creative Visualization Activity Book for Children
Beverly D. Roman
(BR Anchor Publishing)

Why Do We Have to Move?
C. MacGregor

Moving with Children
T. Olkowski

The Moving Book: A Kids' Survival Guide
Gabriel Davis
(Little, Brown)

◆ SOURCES ON MOVING TO THE COUNTRY
Moving to the Country Once and For All
Lisa Rogak
The Complete Country Business Guide
Lisa Rogak
(Williams Hill Publishing)
(603) 523-7877

Country Careers, Jerry Germer
(Wiley)

◆ TAX DEDUCTIONS ON JOB SEARCH AND MOVING
EXPENSES
IRS
(800) 829-1040
www.irs.ustreas.gov

Index

accepting job offer, consequences of, 189–93

acclimatization, to new location, 199–202

accommodations, in target city, 100–101

ACRA *Cost of Living Index*, 19

advertisements for employment, 93
online resources, 214–15
responding to, 78–79

airplane pricing and ticketing, resources, 216, 217

American Association of Advertising Agencies, 37, 213

American Association of Medical Colleges, 37, 213

American Automobile Association (AAA), 99

American Business Information, 31

American Business Information Directory, 29, 208

American Chamber of Commerce Researchers Association, 19, 207

American Manufacturers Directory, 29, 209

America's Job Bank, internet, 42

"America's 10 Most Enlightened Towns," 18

AmeriSuites, 101

annual reports, use of, in job search, 34, 209

appointments, making a list of, 94

"Best Companies for Work and Family," 30, 210

"Best Companies for Working Mothers" (*Working Mother*), 30, 211

best-place-to-work lists, 30, 210, 211

The Big Book of Jobs (VGM), 121, 211

budget, on target city visits, 101

businesses, resources on, 208–11

Business Newsbank, 33, 209

Business Week, 30, 210

career centers, internet, 42

career consultation for spouses, 180

career-related chat rooms, 38, 211–12

CareerXRoads, the 1998 Directory to the 500 Best Job, Résumé and Career Management Sites on the World Wide Web (MMC Group), 38, 42, 43, 212

CD-ROMs, use of, in job search, 29–30

Change of Address form, 193

chat rooms, career-related, 38, 211–12

checklists. *See* worksheets

Cheapskate newsletter, 101

children:
activities/facilities for, in target location, 133–34
effects of moving on, 7–8
resources on moving with, 220
special needs of, upon completion of move, 204

cities and towns, ratings of, 18–20, 207–8

classified advertisements, on internet, 43
clothes, for first business meeting, 111
colleagues in your field, use of, in job search, 38–39
communication skills, 128
commuting partner, 203
company web pages, 42
computer rental, 111
"Consider Relocation," internet site, 42
correspondence, 94
in job search, 57–87
See also letters, sample
cost, of moving, 11, 112, 179–81
cost-of-living, resources on, 207–8
counteroffers, for jobs, 185–87
country, resources on moving to, 220
coworkers, telling them about relocation plans, 66
creating your own position, 123–25, 173
credibility, and job search follow-up, 156–57

databases. *See* internet
decision to move, 3–4, 13–17
Department of Economic Development, 37
Dictionary of Occupational Titles (VGM), 121, 211
The Directory of Executive Recruiters (Kennedy Publications), 40, 213
doubts, about moving, 2–4
Dow Jones Interactive Publishing, 36, 210

Economic Advisory Council, 37
economizing while visiting target location, resources about, 216–17
"emoticons," 38
Employee Benefits Research Institute, 182
employee referral programs, 76–77

Employment Relocation Council, 204
evaluation of first visit to target location, 141–53
excitement, about moving, 10
executive recruiter sources, resources, 213
Expedia.com, 99–100, 216
Extended Stay America, 101
extended-stay hotels, 100–101, 217

family. *See* children; spouses
fear of moving, 10
first impressions, and job search, 62–64
first meeting with referrals in target location, 67–71, 101–9
basic considerations and things to bring, 117–18
clothes for, 111
follow-ups to people you met, 190–91
record of, 95, 96, 97
taking charge of, 105–9
turning into a job interview, 120–23
unsuccessful, 126–28
first visit to target location:
assessment of, upon return home, 137–74
planning, 89–114
strategy/logistics while there, 115–35
flex positions, 131–33
follow-up, 128–29
calls, after letter, 74–76
with first contact people, after accepting an offer, 190–91
in various job search scenarios, 153–62
Fortune magazine, 19, 30, 210
friends of the family, in target location, 77–78

General Business File, 33, 209
getting away from something, as reason for moving, 4–5
giving notice, at old place of employment, 189–90

goals, establishing, in job search, 22–27, 92
gut reaction, to target location, 140–41

headhunters, 39–41. *See also* recruiters
Hilton Garden Inn Hotels, 101, 217
Homestead Village, 101
Hoover's Company Capsules, 35
Hoover's Online, 35, 210
Hoover's Online Library, 35
hotels, 100–101
    resources, 216, 217, 218
human resources professionals and departments, avoiding, 125–26

Interim Services, 132
Internal Revenue Service Publications, moving/job search expenses forms, 191–92
International Association of Conference Centers, 43, 212
International Salary Calculator, web site, 182
internet, 35–39, 42–43, 207–20
    access to, in hotels, 101
    advertisements of employment positions, 214–15
    airplane pricing and ticketing, 216, 217
    chat rooms, 38, 211–12
    companies, information about, 208–11
    cost-of-living guides, 207–8
    flex positions on, 131–33
    hotel resources, 217, 218
    job descriptions, 211
    job search/career resources, 212–13
    and locale questions, 18–19, 28, 207–8
    maps on, 99–100, 216
    moving companies on, 219
    multicultural intern and recruitment programs, 213

pitfalls of use of, in job search, 28–29
    professional organizations on, 42–43
    ratings of hotels, motels, and restaurants, 218
    real estate resources, 219–20
    recruiter sources, 213
    rental car airport rates, 218
    résumé databases, 42, 93, 215
    salary issues, 182
    tax deductions information, 220
    temporary job services, resources on, 131–33, 214
    trade organizations on, 212
    travel information, 216–18
    use of, in job search, 35–39, 42–43
    weather reports/forecasts, 218
internships, 133
Interview Record Forms, 126
interviews. *See* job interviews
introductory letters to people you've never met, 74
ITT Sheraton, 101

job banks, 93
    internet, 42
job descriptions, resources on, 211
job focus groups, 49
job interviews, 110, 129–30
    meetings turning into, 120–23
    See also first meeting with referrals in target location
job offers:
    accepting, consequences of, 189–93
    assessment of whether you want, 175–78
    before you accept, 179–85
    being realistic about, 163–64
    declining, 188
    moving without any, 130–34
    multiple, dealing with, 187–88
    negotiations, 179–87
    responding to, 162–63, 175–98
    sample letters from employers, 195–97
    waiting for, 164–67

job openings, 214–15
  hearing of, 119–20
  resources, 212–15
  where listed, 53–54
job search
  correspondence in, 57–87
  from current home, for target
    location, 21–55
  follow-ups, and credibility, 156–
    57
  internet resources, 212–13
  organizing your data, 90–96
  outcome scenarios, and follow-
    ups, 153–62
  people skills in, 44–55, 57–87
  positioning yourself in, 60–64
  research in, 27–43
  strategy for, 22–27, 92
  See also first visit to target
    location

keeping in touch, sample letter,
  174
Kennedy Publications, 40
Kouzes, James, and Barry Posner,
  Credibility, 157

Laptop Lane, 134
layovers (between planes), using to
  advantage, 134
letters:
  introductory, to people you've
    never met, 74
  to job referrals and potential
    employers, 72–74
letters, sample:
  creating your own position,
    173
  if there are no job openings,
    168
  if you have no contacts at
    company, 170–71
  if you have no offer yet, 172
  if you're not interested, 169
  job offer from employer, 195–97
  keeping in touch, 174
  nagging, to be avoided, 73–74
  new job announcement, 198
  to person you've read about, 86

to recruiter, 87
referral letters, 72–74, 83–84
response to advertisement or
  known position, 85
thank-you, after first meeting,
  108
thank-you, to someone in
  hometown, 82
library, use of, in job search, 29–30
LibrarySpot, 38, 209
listservs, use of, in job search, 38–
  39
livability profile (of place), 14–17
location:
  decision about where to move,
    13–17
  finding out facts about, 17–20
  research resources, 18–19, 207–8
Location Guides, 17–18, 207
Location Report, 17
logistics, of first visit to target
  location, 115–16
lost-wage compensation, 180
low-cost goods, resources about,
  216–17

MainStay, 101
Management Recruiters
  International, 41, 213
maps, 99–100, 216
Marriott, 101, 217
mass mailings, use of, in job search,
  31, 40
meetings. *See* first meeting with
  referrals in target location; job
  interviews
Money magazine, 18–19, 207
Move Mantra, 93
  expanding upon, 103–5
  sample, 62–65
moving:
  clarifying reasons for, 5–6
  cost of, 11, 112, 179–81
  emotions about, 8–10
  without any job offers, 130–34
moving companies, 192–93, 219
moving day, 193
Multicultural Advertising Intern
  Program, 37

Multicultural Intern and Recruitment Programs, resources, 213

National Trade & Professional Associations of the United States (Columbia Books), 43, 212
negotiations, about a job offer, 179–87
NETSHARE, 42
networking, vs. building sincere relationships, 45–47
newsgroups, use of, in job search, 38
newsletters, use of, in job search, 34
newspapers:
    classified advertisements of, on internet, 43
    use of, in job search, 31–33
noncompete contracts, 183–85
"normal" vs. "abnormal," avoid labeling oneself as, 54–55
"North America's Most Improved Cities," 19

"100 Best Companies to Work for in America, The" (Fortune magazine), 30, 210
O*Net Dictionary of Occupational Titles, The (JIST), 121, 211
online resources. See internet
optional working arrangements, 131–33

packing, for first visit, 111
partners. See spouses
part-time work, 203. See also temporary employment
pen pals, 204
people contacts:
    in job search, 57–87
    protocol/etiquette with, 44–45
Places Rated Almanac, 18
positioning, in job search, 60–64
prioritizing:
    in decision to move, 3–4
    environmental factors of location, 15–17

Professional Convention Management Association, 43, 212
professional meetings, meeting people at, in job search, 49
professional organizations, internet sites, 42–43
pros and cons of moving, 6–7
protocol/etiquette, with people in job search, 44–45
publications, use of, in job search, 31–34
public postings of positions, 28
    vs. proactive job search, 53

questions, asking, in first job search meeting, 107

ratings:
    best-place-to-work lists, 30, 210, 211
    of cities and towns, 18–20, 207–8
    of hotels, motels, and restaurants, 218
reactions:
    to first visit to target location, 137–38
    predicting, of people you contact in job search, 59–61
real estate and realtors:
    meeting with, on first visit to target location, 133
    resources about, 219–20
reasons for moving, 1–6
recreational activities, in target location, 133–34
recruiters, 39–41
    internet resources, 213
    letters to, 87
referrals, 70, 71–72, 94, 118–19
    asking for, in first job search meeting, 107
    asking for, prematurely, 127–28
reimbursement, for trip, by target company, 112
relocation expenses, 11, 112, 179–81
relocation packets, from realtors, 133

reneging on job offer, 188
rental cars, 99
   airport rates online, 218
research, 92–93
   on job search, 27–43
   keeping a list of topics to
      research, 93
   resources, 207–12
resentment, about move, 8–9
Residence Inns, 101, 217
resources, 17, 207–20
restrictive covenants, 183–85
résumés:
   copies of, 95
   dissemination of, 93
   internet databases, 42, 93, 215
Roman, Beverly, *Runzheimer
   Reports on Relocation*, 7
Runzheimer International, 11, 207

salary issues, 181–82
schools, investigating, in target
   location, 133–34
services, low-cost, resources about,
   216–17
severance package, if job doesn't
   work out, 182–83
shy people, job search of, 54–55
sightseeing, in target locations, 133–
   34
simultaneous tasks, managing, 51–
   54
SiteNet, 36–37, 210
Site Selection Magazine, 36–37
spouses:
   career consultation for, 180
   commuting, 203
   effects of moving on, 8–10
   relocation programs for, 112
   unemployed or underemployed,
      202–3
Standard & Poor's Register, 29–30,
   209
Staybridge Suites, 101
strategy, for job search, 22–27, 92
stress, at new location, 199

taking charge, of first job search
   meeting, 105–9

target companies, 93
Target Company List, 95, 117
Target Company Profile, form, 95–
   96, 98–99
target location
   accommodations in, 100–101
   actual move to, strategies and
      logistics of acclimatizing to,
      199–205
   friends of the family in, 77–78
   gut reaction to, 140–41
   meeting people there on pre-
      move job search, 71–72
   sightseeing in, 133–34
   See also visits
tax deductions, 191–92
   resources on, 220
telephoning, in job search, 57–87
temporary employment
   ("temping"), 131–33, 203
   online resources, 131–33, 214
thank-you notes, 70, 82, 108, 130
Thomas Register, 35–36, 210
three-minute commercial (about
   self), 104–7
trade magazines, use of, in job
   search, 34
trade organizations, resources on,
   212
travel:
   internet resources, 216–18
   local, in target location, 116–17
   to and from target location, 99
   while at target location, 99–100

unemployed or underemployed
   partner, 202–3
U.S. Big Business Directory, 29, 208
Utne Reader, 18

vacillation, about moving, 2–4
Vault Reports, 36, 210
videotapes, about places, 17
visits:
   initial. *See* first visit to target
      location
   planning second, 160–61

waiting for job offers, 164–67
The Wall Street Journal, Interactive Edition, 42, 214
weather sources, online, 218
web sites. *See* internet
Working Mother, 30, 211
worksheets and checklists:
   evaluation of first visit to target location, 141–53
   first visit things to accomplish, 114
   goals and strategies, 27
   people to talk to about job search, 48–51
   reasons for moving, 5–6, 12
   Target Company Profile, 95–99
   "What's Important to Me," regarding location, 16–17